The Creator's Blueprint

By

David Toliver

This book is a work of nonfiction. The information contained herein is provided for educational and inspirational purposes only. The author and publisher assume no responsibility for errors or omissions, or for outcomes related to the application of the material.

For permissions or inquiries, please contact:

Theempoweredcreators@gmail.com

Reader Acknowledgement

The *Creator's Blueprint* is an additional resource meant to be used alongside *Creativity Is Currency: How To Turn Your Ideas Into Wealth*, which is a motivational and educational resource designed to inspire personal transformation, creative empowerment, and entrepreneurial action. The strategies, methods, and concepts shared in this book are based on the author's experience, research, and perspective.

While this book provides powerful tools and insights for personal and financial growth, it does not guarantee specific results. Every reader's journey is different. Your success depends on many factors, including your background, effort, commitment, mindset, and timing.

This book is not a substitute for financial, legal, medical, or psychological advice. Please consult the appropriate licensed professional before making any significant changes in these areas.

Editor Acknowledgement

I would like to extend my deepest gratitude to my editor, Emmanuel, whose exceptional skill and insight helped shape this book into its best form. Emmanuel not only honored the vision I carried for this work, but also elevated it. Emmanuel refined the book while preserving its heart and purpose. From the beginning, Emmanuel demonstrated a clear understanding of my goals, offering constructive guidance that never compromised my voice. His editorial precision and thoughtful suggestions made a tremendous impact on the clarity, flow, and effectiveness of every chapter. It was a true collaboration marked by professionalism, integrity, and excellence. I am sincerely grateful for his dedication to this project. Emmanuel, your contribution will always be part of the foundation of *Creativity Is Currency* and additional resources such as this blueprint. It was an honor to work with you. I am sure we will continue a long working relationship, as we give God all the Glory!

– **David Toliver**

Earnings Disclaimer

Any case studies, income examples, or business outcomes discussed in this book are not promises or guarantees of results. They are shared for educational purposes only. There is no assurance you will earn any income by simply reading or applying the methods in this book. Any financial success or transformation you achieve will be the result of your own dedication, consistency, and actions.

Author Disclaimer

I, David Toliver, author of *The Creator's Blueprint*, make every effort to ensure the accuracy of the information presented in this book. However, the content is provided "as is" and without warranties of any kind, either expressed or implied. I assume no responsibility or liability for any errors, omissions, or outcomes that may arise from applying the content of this book.

This book is written to educate, uplift, and encourage creativity and self-leadership. It is not intended to replace personalized coaching, counseling, legal services, or business advice from qualified professionals. You are responsible for your own choices and outcomes.

By reading this book, you agree to take full responsibility for your personal and business decisions.

Table of Contents

Welcome To The Journey Of Your Creative Power 9

Creativity Is Currency Bonus Material Helps You Apply What You Learn 10

Wealth Idea Builder Sheet 10

25 Plug-And-Play Wealth Idea Starters 13

Power Statement Builder 16

25 Ways To Use Your Power Statement 18

Your Progress Tracker & Your Assessment 24

"Show Me The Wall" – The Creative Wealth Builder Blueprint 27

25 Bricks (Concepts To Build With): 28

"Wall Builder" Checklist: 30

How To Use This Poster: 30

Motivational Quote (From The Book): 31

Elevator Pitch Builder: Step-By-Step System 31

50 Elevator Pitch Concepts To Practice 33

Part 1: Launch Planning Template 36

Part 2: Income Stream Tracker 38

Part 3: 50 Ideas To Use The Launch Planning Template + Income Tracker 39

Chapter One

Creativity Activation **.......... *42***

"Unstuck: Your Power Plan To Break Through And Build Forward" 42

Section One: The Power Of Breakthrough Mindsets 42

Section Two: Action Over Obstacles 43

Progress Tracker 47

25 Practical Strategies To Activate "What's In Your Hands Today" 48

Chapter Two

Wisdom Tracker: The Path To Purposeful Decisions **.......... *56***

Part One: The Wisdom–Vision Connection 56

Part Two: Daily Wisdom PracticeMood Check-In: 57

Part Three: Decision-Making Checklist 57

Part Four: Daily Wisdom Score 58

Part Five: Weekly Wisdom Reflection 59

Bonus: Wisdom Growth Chart (Track Weekly Scores) 60

25 Key Strategies To Create, Build, And Prosper With Wisdom 63

Chapter Three

Become The Person Blueprint **.......... *68***

Purpose Of This Blueprint 68

Daily Mindset Reset 69

Identity Alignment Tracker 69
Action Steps To Become 70
Who You'Re Becoming 72
Visual Transformation Framework: From Struggling To Strong & Successful 73
Building The Person You Must Become 76
Final Thought: 81
Call To Action 81

Chapter Four

Chapter Four: Build Your Financial Wisdom 82

What Is Financial Wisdom—And Why It Matters 85
Visual Framework: "The Financial Wisdom Diamond" 86
Deeper Wisdom Principles 86
Benchmark: Where Am I Now? 89
Call To Action: What You Must Do Now 90
Deeper Wisdom Principles 90
Where Am I Now? 93
What Kind Of Advisor Do You Need? 93
Call To Action: What You Must Do Now 98

Chapter Five *99*

Legacy Builder Blueprint *99*

Bonus: Legacy Accountability Partner **114**

Chapter Six

What Your Hand Findeth To Do, Do It With All Your Might *115*

25 Practical Daily Execution Strategies: 123

Suggested Tracking Tools: 127

Chapter Six Wrap-Up Commitment 129

Chapter Seven

Legacy Giving Blueprint *129*

What Is Legacy Giving? 129

25 Ways To Use The Brand Clarity Map 136

Bonus Chapter: Creativity Is Currency – The Armor Of Riches And Wealth145

The Six Pieces Of Armor — A Complete Overview 145

Armor Of Riches And Wealth 150

The Outcome: 153

The Wealth Warrior's Commitment 154

A Compelling Thought: 168

Legacy Builder Blueprint 168

Diamond Of Legacy Framework 173

Creativity Is Currency: Do It With All Your Might Activation 174

Appendix: Tools, Resources & Study Aids 180

Welcome to the Journey of Your Creative Power

Dear Reader,

I want to begin with one powerful truth: **you were born with something the world needs.**

This book, *The Creator's Blueprint* helps you apply what you learn. It was written for **you**—the visionary, the dreamer, the hard worker with bold ideas who's tired of watching others succeed while wondering, *"When will it be my time?"*

Your time is now.

This is not just a book you read, it's a movement you step into. It's a call to rise, create, build, and own your path to freedom and fulfillment. This book was created with your story in mind. Maybe you've tried before and felt stuck. Perhaps you've been overwhelmed by life, plagued by self-doubt, or faced with limited opportunities. But here's the message I want to leave imprinted on your soul:

You are the creator of your next chapter.

Inside these pages, you will discover how to activate the power already in your hands. You'll learn how to:

- Unlock your creativity as a tool for influence and income.
- Develop a mindset that attracts wealth, not just riches.

- Turn your ideas into products, services, and solutions people will pay for.
- Build something that outlives your legacy.

This book speaks directly to your capacity to create change. It will walk you through **real frameworks** and **actionable strategies**—no fluff. The book will challenge you to think differently, plan intentionally, and act with courage. Each chapter will guide you through reflective prompts, step-by-step systems, and powerful inspiration to help you stay focused.

Creativity Is Currency Bonus Material Helps You Apply What You Learn

To support your journey, I've created a library of **tools** just for you:

- **What's in your hands today?**
- **How does wisdom shape your daily decisions?**
- **Building the person I must become**
- What kind of advisor do you need?
- **Generational Wealth Assessment**
- **Daily Execution Map**
- Who am I called to bless
- **Bonus: The Armor of Riches and Wealth**

These tools were designed to **help you take immediate action**, stay accountable, and see actual results in your business and life.

Wealth Idea Builder Sheet

"Start – Sketch – System"

STEP 1: START (THE SEED)

Objective: Clarify the value-driven idea you want to turn into income.

- **What problem are you solving?**
- **Who needs this solution?**
- **What knowledge, skill, or insight do you already have that supports this idea?**
- **Why are you passionate about solving this problem?**

STEP 2: SKETCH (THE BLUEPRINT)

Objective: Visualize the shape and impact of your idea.

- **Describe your offer in one sentence:**
  (Ex: "I help overwhelmed new entrepreneurs start a business with clarity and confidence in 30 days.")
- **What are the three outcomes someone will achieve from this idea?**

1. ______________________________

2. ______________________________

3. ______________________________

- **What form will your idea take?**
  (Check one or more)
  - Online Course
  - Digital Download
  - Consulting or Coaching
  - Booklet or eBook
  - Workshop or Masterclass
  - Service/Done-for-you Offer
  - Membership Program
  - Physical Product

- **What does success look like for your customer?**

STEP 3: SYSTEM (THE STRUCTURE)

Objective: Turn your idea into a system that consistently produces value and income.

- **List your 3–5 steps to deliver the transformation:**

1. ______________________________

2. ______________________________

3. ______________________________

4.____

5.____

- **What system will ensure this offer remains repeatable and scalable?**
  (Ex: templates, frameworks, automations, client journeys, etc.)
- **What price will you charge? Why?**
- **What are your estimated monthly sales goals from this idea?**
- **How will you track success or performance?**

- Revenue

- Customer feedback

- Testimonials

- Growth in followers/audience

- Repeat clients or referrals

25 Plug-and-Play Wealth Idea Starters

1. Teach a skill you've mastered (public speaking, writing, investing)

2. Turn your life story into a motivational masterclass

3. Offer leadership coaching to emerging professionals

4. Help small businesses create interesting branding

5. Guide first-time authors through self-publishing

6. Sell digital templates for productivity or goal-setting
7. Start a lifestyle blog with monetized affiliate links
8. Create a weekly wisdom email newsletter with paid tiers
9. Launch a course on building generational wealth
10. Develop a confidence coaching program for teens
11. Offer content strategy services for authors/creatives
12. Sell merchandise with empowering affirmations
13. Lead faith-based entrepreneurship workshops
14. Provide financial literacy coaching
15. Help creatives protect their intellectual property
16. Build a podcast about creative business breakthroughs
17. Design a budgeting system for creators and dreamers
18. Build an "idea incubator" group coaching community
19. Create a vision board + goal-planner product bundle
20. Host a retreat for legacy-minded leaders
21. Create a done-for-you course creation service
22. Design a planner based on the "Armor of Wealth" system
23. Develop a 21-day "Creativity Is Currency" challenge
24. Offer storytelling workshops for business owners

25. Curate a library of inspirational digital posters or art

This Book Is Your Blueprint

By the end of this book, you won't just be informed—you will **transform**.

You'll have a new mindset. A new vision. And a clear path forward to use what's already in your hands—your creativity—to build the life, business, and legacy you were born to own.

So, let's get started. Not someday. Not when everything's perfect. Not when the timing feels right.

Start today—because what's in you is greater than what's behind you.

You are not alone. I believe in you.

Let's build something that matters.

With gratitude,
David Toliver
Founder & Author of *The Creator's Blueprint*

POWER STATEMENT BUILDER

Purpose: To help you craft a powerful personal or business statement that reflects their unique creativity, value, and mission in a way that motivates action and builds momentum.

STEP 1: IDENTIFY YOUR CORE

Q: What do you believe in?

- Example: "I believe everyone has a gift that can change the world."

Q: What motivates you to act?

- Example: "I'm driven to help others unlock their potential and turn ideas into income."

STEP 2: DEFINE YOUR IMPACT

Q: Who do you serve or want to help?

- Example: "I serve aspiring entrepreneurs with untapped creativity."

Q: What problem do you solve for them?

- Example: "I help them gain clarity, build a product, and create income from their ideas."

STEP 3: CLARIFY YOUR METHOD

Q: How do you help?

- Example: "Through coaching, tools, and workshops rooted in faith, creativity, and business systems."

Q: What makes your approach different?

- Example: "My framework blends creative ownership with mindset transformation and wealth-building principles."

STEP 4: CRAFT YOUR POWER STATEMENT

Format:
"I help [WHO] who struggle with [PROBLEM] by [SOLUTION/METHOD] so they can [RESULT]."

Example Statement:

"I help purpose-driven individuals who feel stuck in their creativity to turn their ideas into income by using my 'Creativity Is Currency' method so that they can build wealth, freedom, and legacy."

Power Statement Builder Template

Use this space to write your own:

- **Who I help**:
- **The problem they face**:
- **How I solve it**:
- **The results I have helped them achieve**:

MY POWER STATEMENT:

"I help ___________________ who struggle with ________________ by

_____________________ so they can ______________________."

25 WAYS TO USE YOUR POWER STATEMENT

1. Add it to your **website homepage** or "About Me" section.
2. Use it as your **LinkedIn bio** or summary.
3. Post it on **your Instagram and Facebook bios**.
4. Use it as your **email signature line**.
5. Start your **YouTube or podcast intro** with it.
6. Print it on **your business card**.
7. Use it to **introduce yourself at networking events**.
8. Speak it aloud in front of the mirror to **boost confidence**.
9. Add it to your **elevator pitch** during sales calls.

10. Include it in your **press kit or media kit**.
11. Turn it into a **video reel** and share online.
12. Use it to **guide your content topics**.
13. Post it on your **office wall or vision board**.
14. Create a **PDF lead magnet** around it.
15. Use it to clarify your **product or service offerings**.
16. Share it during the intro to a masterclass.
17. Teach others how to write theirs and build trust.
18. Use it to **overcome impostor syndrome**.
19. Include it in a **book preface** or back cover.
20. Begin your **next business plan or pitch deck** with it.
21. Use it as a tagline for your coaching or consulting business.
22. Say it in your **morning affirmations or prayer journal**.
23. Use it to vet new **partnerships or opportunities**.
24. Include it in **your product packaging or labels**.
25. Anchor your **legacy and brand identity** in this statement.

THE VISUAL WEALTH BLUEPRINT

Subtitle: Turn Your Creativity into Ownership, Value, and Generational Wealth

---

Step-by-Step Wealth Creation Path

At the center of this blueprint is the creator — **YOU** — and surrounding you are the **6 Core Pillars of Creative Wealth**:

Center: You — The Creator

- You are the idea generator, the innovator, the visionary.
- You activate each area by applying what's in your hands and mind.

---

1. Mindset Mastery

- **Focus:** Shift from survival to strategy.
- **Action:** Adopt a wealth identity.
- **Tool:** Daily affirmations, journal prompts, vision statement.
- **Benchmark:** Replace limiting beliefs with empowering ones.

---

2. Value Identification

- **Focus:** What problem can you solve?
- **Action:** Identify your unique genius and skill set.
- **Tool:** Problem-to-solution.
- **Benchmark:** Pinpoint at least one profitable idea from personal experience.

---

3. Idea Monetization

- **Focus:** Package your creativity into a product or service.
- **Action:** Start simply by offering coaching, a course, or a digital download.
- **Tool:** Product creation canvas.
- **Benchmark:** One offer mapped and priced.

---

4. Brand & Identity

- **Focus:** Who are you to your audience?
- **Action:** Build visual identity and brand story.
- **Tool:** Brand Clarity Framework.
- **Benchmark:** Logo, tagline, elevator pitch, mission, and offer.

---

5. Marketing & Promotion

- **Focus:** Attract and communicate with your people.
- **Action:** Develop marketing content and plan.
- **Tool:** Content calendar, hook-generator, and funnels.
- **Benchmark:** First 30 days of content mapped out.

---

6. Revenue & Protection

- **Focus:** Turn income into wealth and protect it.
- **Action:** Diversify income, track earnings, and use protection strategies.
- **Tool:** Revenue Streams Tracker, Financial Shield Planner.
- **Benchmark:** Identify 3+ revenue streams and one legal protection step (LLC, trademark, insurance, etc.)

---

25 Key Concepts to Apply the Visual Wealth Blueprint

1. **Own your story** – turn your journey into transformation for others.
2. **Think legacy, not hustle** – build something that outlives you.
3. **Identify one skill** you can teach, offer, or package.
4. **Write a vision statement** that aligns with your financial goals.
5. **Solving problems** before selling — money follows solutions.
6. **Choose one ideal customer** — be specific.
7. **Package your offer** using what you already know.
8. **Brand yourself visually** — logo, color palette, typography.
9. **Create your "signature message." What** do you stand for?
10. **Clarify your pricing model** — be confident in charging what you're worth.
11. **Launch a digital product** (eBook, worksheet, webinar).
12. **Create a small lead magnet funnel (e.g.,** PDF, quiz, guide).
13. **Use storytelling in all marketing efforts.**

14. **Develop five brand values and incorporate them into** your messaging.
15. **Establish a weekly financial tracking habit**.
16. **Start a YouTube channel or podcast** to share your method.
17. **Protect your ideas** legally (IP, trademarks).
18. **Test and pivot** — your first idea doesn't have to be perfect.
19. **Build a relationship-first business.**
20. **Collaborate with aligned communities or partners.**
21. **Set 90-day outcome goals.**
22. **Measure what matters** — focus on impact, not vanity metrics.
23. **Create recurring-income products.**
24. **Celebrate progress publicly.**
25. **Stay rooted in purpose and faith** — never forget your "why."

Your Initial Call to Action

"Wealth is not built by chance — it's built by design. The moment you realize that you can own your creativity is the moment you stop waiting and start becoming. Use this blueprint to take bold action. Build your brand. Own your value. Share your voice. Create a legacy that multiplies."

Your Progress Tracker & Your Assessment

Empowering you to take bold, creative steps with clarity, courage, and measurable progress.

PART 1: Step-by-Step Tracker Framework

Step	Milestone	Action to Take	Reflection	Status
1.	Clarity of Vision	Complete "What's in Your Hands" inventory	What do you currently have that you can use?	Not Yet / In Progress / Done
2.	Unlock Creativity	Write down three creative ideas you've had in the past month	Which idea excites you most? Why?	
3.	Ownership Mindset	List three self-limiting beliefs and rewrite them with truth statements	How do you now feel about your potential?	
4.	Marketable Idea	Choose one creative idea and validate it with a potential audience	What feedback did you receive?	
5.	Branding	Define your message,	What does your	

Step	Milestone	Action to Take	Reflection	Status
	Basics	mission, and identity	brand stand for?	
6.	Value Creation	Identify the exact problem your creativity solves	What transformation do you offer others?	
7.	Product/Offer	Sketch your first product, service, or solution	What will people pay you for?	
8.	Revenue Strategy	Determine at least two ways your product/service can generate income	Which is most aligned with your goals?	
9.	Marketing System	Create a list of platforms to promote your offer	Where does your audience hang out?	
10.	Confidence to Launch	Write a declaration to own your creativity	What will you do this week to move forward?	

PART 2: Your Assessment

Rate each from 1 (not at all) to 5 (entirely accurate):

1. I have a clear vision of what I want to create.

2. I believe my ideas are valuable and marketable.

3. I know how to take ownership of my creativity.

4. I feel confident in turning ideas into income.

5. I've defined my brand identity and message.

6. I consistently learn from and apply the insights in the book.

7. I know who my audience is and how to reach them.

8. I've started building or offering a product or service.

9. I can confidently communicate the value I bring.

10. I've developed the mindset to persevere through tough times.

Total Score:
40–50: You're ready to launch with power!
30–39: You're building momentum. Keep going!
20–29: You've got the pieces — time to organize and focus.
Under 20: Time to take bold actions now.

PART 3: 25 Ways to Use This Tracker & Assessment

1. Reflect weekly on your progress and adjust your goals accordingly.
2. Use it as a journal to deepen self-awareness.
3. Pair it with workbook prompts after each chapter.
4. Bring it to group coaching sessions for feedback.
5. Share it with a trusted friend or accountability partner.
6. Review it monthly to track actual growth.

7. Track emotional progress — not just tasks.
8. Use it before launching your first product or service.
9. Mark key obstacles and document how you overcame them.
10. Add visuals (mood boards, branding, logo ideas).
11. Turn each step into a goal for a weekly challenge.
12. Use it as a teaching tool when mentoring others.
13. Create a vision board based on your answers.
14. Review annually and celebrate progress.
15. Document new creative ideas sparked by reflection.
16. Add benchmarks and deadlines to keep yourself accountable.
17. Establish a reward system for completing significant milestones.
18. Track testimonials and feedback you receive.
19. Use the results to shape your next big idea.
20. Compare your mindset now to where you began.
21. Use it during a business or creative retreat.
22. Display your favorite progress milestones visually.
23. Create a private "Creativity Is Currency" group and share.
24. Highlight action steps and track income growth.
25. Use it as proof of your transformation!

"Show Me the Wall" – The Creative Wealth Builder Blueprint

A step-by-step motivational visual guide for building wealth from your creativity.

POSTER DESIGN LAYOUT: See if you can create this Wall?

At the top center:
"Show Me the Wall"
Tagline: Build it. See it. Live it.

Visual layout:
A large central wall (brick layout or blueprint style) with **25 bricks**. Each brick contains a concept, principle, or action from the book *Creativity Is Currency*. At the base of the wall, the foundation is titled **"Your Why"**, and the top brick is **"Your Legacy."**

On the right: A checklist.
On the left: A motivational quote from the book.

At the bottom: A space for your photo or affirmation.

---

25 BRICKS (CONCEPTS TO BUILD WITH):

Each of these is a **foundational idea** that turns into a habit, skill, or identity as you build your personal and professional "wall" of success.

1. Define Your Why

2. Believe You Are the Creator

3. Activate the Creator Mindset

4. Write One Wealth-Building Idea

5. Identify Your Skill Set

6. Turn Problems into Opportunities

7. Build Your Brand Identity

8. Name Your Product or Service

9. Clarify Your Message

10. Visualize Your Audience

11. Create a Signature Offer

12. Validate Your Solution

13. Launch Your First Offer

14. Master Your Finances

15. Track All Revenue Streams

16. Build Influence & Visibility

17. Protect Your Assets & Ideas

18. Refine Your Daily Systems

19. Measure What Matters

20. Strengthen Your Mindset

21. Surround Yourself with Builders

22. Reinvest in Your Growth

23. Serve with Excellence

24. Inspiration & Uplift Others

25. **Own Your Creativity Daily**

"WALL BUILDER" CHECKLIST:

- I know my why
- I created a brand message
- I identified a revenue stream
- I made a public offer
- I tracked sales or audience growth
- I developed a product or service
- I solved one problem for someone
- I reinvested in my growth
- I journaled my progress
- I decided with wisdom
- I showed up consistently
- I reminded myself, "I am a Creator."

HOW TO USE THIS POSTER:

1. **Place this where you see it daily**: In your office, bedroom, or creative space.
2. **Choose one brick per day or week** to focus on.
3. **Reflect**: What have I built today?
4. **Mark each concept complete** as you embody it.

5. **Write a date at the top** when your wall was first started and your projected legacy date.

MOTIVATIONAL QUOTE (From the Book):

"You are not waiting for the wall to be built — you are the builder. Your creativity is the brick. Your belief is the mortar. Now build."

Elevator Pitch Builder: Step-by-Step System

This framework empowers you to communicate who you are, what you do, and why it matters—in 60 seconds or less. Perfect for networking, pitching ideas, selling products, or introducing their brand.

STEP-BY-STEP: THE CREATIVITY IS CURRENCY ELEVATOR PITCH BUILDER

STEP 1: WHO ARE YOU? (Identity)

Describe who you are and your core role in 1–2 lines.

"Hi, my name is David. I'm a creative entrepreneur and the founder of [your company/product name]."

STEP 2: WHAT DO YOU DO? (Value Proposition)
Briefly explain the key solution you offer.

"I help people turn their creativity into real, profitable ideas that build legacy and wealth."

STEP 3: WHO DO YOU HELP? (Audience)
Clarify your target market or audience.

"I work with aspiring entrepreneurs, creatives, and professionals who feel stuck but know they're meant for more."

STEP 4: WHAT PROBLEM DO YOU SOLVE? (Pain Point)
State the primary issue your audience is facing.

"Most people don't know how to monetize their ideas or where to start, and they stay overwhelmed or underpaid."

STEP 5: WHAT IS THE PROMISE OR TRANSFORMATION? (Outcome)
Share the result or success story your product/service/book delivers.

"My book shows you how to unlock your ideas, build wealth, and walk in purpose by owning their creativity."

STEP 6: CALL TO ACTION (CTA)
End with a clear invitation to connect, learn more, or take the next step.

"If you're ready to take the next step, I'd love for you to check out my masterclass or grab a copy of the book."

50 Elevator Pitch Concepts to Practice

Below are 50 concepts you can use to apply the Elevator Pitch Builder framework and craft their unique message depending on their role, audience, and creative work:

CREATIVE INDUSTRY & PERSONAL BRAND

1. A visual artist building a collection and teaching others online
2. A spoken-word poet launching a podcast for healing stories
3. A fashion designer promoting a culturally inspired line
4. A photographer offering branding shoots for entrepreneurs
5. A singer releasing inspirational music on digital platforms
6. A sculptor who teaches inner-city youth how to monetize art
7. A voice actor creating a story-driven audio series
8. A video editor helping small businesses with content
9. A jewelry maker building an e-commerce empire
10. A calligrapher launching a course on creative lettering

ENTREPRENEURSHIP & BUSINESS IDEAS

11. A business coach who helps others build a side hustle
12. A product designer turning ideas into physical goods
13. A digital marketer teaching creators how to grow
14. A copywriter selling brand storytelling services

15. A web developer offering custom design for thought leaders
16. A startup founder launching an app for mental wellness
17. A wellness coach turning journaling into income
18. A course creator teaching a profitable life skill
19. A branding expert offering 1-on-1 personal brand sessions
20. A nonprofit founder raising funds for social impact

THOUGHT LEADERSHIP & INFLUENCE

21. A life coach empowering people through creative belief
22. A speaker teaching courage in business and life
23. A faith-based leader mentoring creatives through mindset
24. A financial coach helping creators manage money
25. A productivity coach helping women launch businesses
26. A DEI consultant integrating creativity into corporate culture
27. A teen mentor using digital storytelling to empower youth
28. A trauma survivor building a movement of healing
29. A retired professional launching a legacy brand
30. A mompreneur empowering others to build from home

EDUCATION & AUTHORSHIP

31. A teacher selling digital curriculum online
32. A writer self-publishing books that uplift and educate
33. A historian teaching culture through storytelling

34. A college student building a passion-led platform
35. A homeschool parent building an education business
36. A speaker launching a TED-style youth event
37. A podcast host monetizing meaningful conversations
38. A curriculum developer selling workshops
39. A blogger turning content into coaching
40. A retired educator creating a creative learning community

CORPORATE & PROFESSIONAL SPACES

41. A corporate leader launching a coaching firm
42. A consultant helping companies innovate with creativity
43. An HR executive launching an employee engagement program
44. A project manager offering planning systems for entrepreneurs
45. A UX designer building tools for the creator economy
46. A real estate agent launching a creative media channel
47. A health worker launching a self-care community
48. A tech entrepreneur making innovation accessible
49. A sales trainer teaching creative pitch techniques
50. A brand strategist launching a visual identity agency

PART 1: LAUNCH PLANNING TEMPLATE

This structured template guides you in planning and executing the launch of an idea, product, or service, utilizing their creative assets.

Step 1: Identify the Idea (What's in Your Hands?)

- What skill, knowledge, or passion are you launching?
- Who is your audience?
- What problem are you solving?

Example: I'm launching a masterclass to teach creators how to turn ideas into digital income.

Step 2: Set Your Launch Objective

- Goal: (ex., Enroll 50 students)
- Deadline: (ex., 30 days from today)
- Target Revenue: (ex., $10,000 from this launch)

Step 3: Prepare Your Launch Assets

Asset	Status	Notes
Landing Page	☐ Ready	
Email Sequence	☐ Ready	5-part launch email series
Social Media Graphics	☐ Ready	Carousel posts, reels, promos
Lead Magnet	☐ Ready	Free PDF download, webinar invite
Webinar or Live Event	☐ Ready	Platform: Zoom / YouTube
Payment Integration	☐ Ready	Stripe or PayPal linked

Step 4: 7-Day Pre-Launch Plan

Day	Task
1.	Teaser post + email to warm list
2.	Launch landing page & lead magnet.
3.	Go live with value content.
4.	Email: "What's Coming Next"
5.	Testimonial/review post
6.	Reminder email + countdown
7.	Masterclass Day or Open Cart

Step 5: Post-Launch Evaluation

- How many leads did you get?
- What was your conversion rate?
- What feedback did you receive?
- What will you improve next time?

PART 2: INCOME STREAM TRACKER

This is a flexible tool for monitoring multiple revenue streams from your creative ventures.

Revenue Stream	Launch Date	Monthly Target	Current Revenue	Notes
Digital Book Sales	6/15/2025	$2,000	$_______	
Masterclass / Webinar	6/20/2025	$3,000	$_______	
Coaching Program	7/01/2025	$5,000	$_______	
Affiliate Partnerships	6/25/2025	$500	$_______	
Speaking Engagements	8/01/2025	$1,500	$_______	
Product Merch / Apparel	7/15/2025	$1,000	$_______	

Revenue Stream	Launch Date	Monthly Target	Current Revenue	Notes
Subscription / Membership	7/10/2025	$2,000	$______	
Online Course	8/01/2025	$3,500	$______	
Consulting Services	7/20/2025	$4,000	$______	
Licensing / IP Use	9/01/2025	$1,000	$______	

PART 3: 50 IDEAS TO USE THE LAUNCH PLANNING TEMPLATE + INCOME TRACKER

1. Write and sell an eBook.
2. Host a paid workshop.
3. Create a members-only content vault.
4. Launch a podcast with sponsorship.
5. Sell branded apparel or journals.
6. Offer a mastermind group.
7. Develop a productivity planner.
8. Sell digital art or templates.
9. Host a retreat.
10. Create a YouTube channel with monetization capabilities.
11. Offer Instagram strategy sessions.
12. Build and sell Canva templates.
13. Sell motivational wall posters.

14. Create a mobile app for goal setting.
15. Design flashcards or affirmation decks.
16. Teach a creativity bootcamp.
17. Offer ghostwriting services.
18. Host writing challenges.
19. Develop a guided journal series.
20. Launch a faith-based business devotional.
21. License your course to schools or organizations.
22. Teach storytelling for entrepreneurs.
23. Offer financial wellness classes.
24. Publish a workbook + bonus training video.
25. Offer text-based coaching.
26. Create a paid community on Circle or Mighty Networks.
27. Launch a revenue share partnership.
28. Start a "Creator's Incubator."
29. Develop monthly themes + paid challenges.
30. Teach a skill you mastered (video editing, branding).
31. Sell lesson plans or curriculum kits.
32. Host a weekly show on Facebook/Instagram Live.
33. Build an online summit.
34. License your intellectual property.
35. Offer a newsletter sponsorship.
36. Create an NFT-based artwork or license.
37. Host a creative journaling workshop.
38. Start a publishing agency.
39. Create a gratitude challenge or devotional.
40. Offer done-for-you service packages.

41. Launch a workbook club.
42. Offer group coaching intensives.
43. Host a live online launch event.
44. Sell a print version of your digital product.
45. Create a quiz funnel that leads to an offer.
46. Design a printable goal map.
47. Launch a parenting/youth version of your concept.
48. Start a Creator Speaker Series.
49. Build a "done-with-you" business accelerator.
50. Launch a "Creativity Is Currency" kit.

Chapter One

Creativity Activation

"Unstuck: Your Power Plan to Break Through and Build Forward"

A Companion to **Creativity Is Currency**

Purpose

This is designed to provide practical solutions to the most common emotional, financial, mental, and strategic challenges that you face on your journey to achieving wealth and personal success. It addresses the *"I'm stuck, now what?"* moments and transforms them into *"I'm empowered, I can do this."*

SECTION ONE: THE POWER OF BREAKTHROUGH MINDSETS

Motivational Thought:

"You are not behind—you are simply being prepared. When you decide to move forward, life will meet you there."

Task: Identify the Limiting Belief

Write down one thought that's been holding you back:

- I'm not ready because...
- I can't afford it because...
- I don't know how because...

Rewrite the Narrative:

- I *am* ready because...
- I *can* afford the first step by...
- I *will* learn how by...

SECTION TWO: ACTION OVER OBSTACLES

Concern #1: Procrastination

Why it happens: Fear of failure, overwhelm, unclear direction
Solution:

- Break down your goal into **three tasks** you can do **this week**
- Use the **"20-Minute Rule"** – Work on a task for just 20 minutes at a time.

Activity:

Create a simple to-do list for this week:

Task	Time Needed	Day to Start
Write down 3 product ideas	30 min	Monday
Research my market	1 hr	Tuesday
Create a basic logo concept	45 min	Thursday

Concern #2: Fear of Failure

Why it happens: Perfectionism, past mistakes, fear of judgment
Solution: Reframe failure as **information**

- Journal 3 "failures" that taught you something powerful

Journal Prompt:

- What didn't go as planned?
- What did I learn?
- How will I apply that insight now?

Concern #3: Lack of Time or Energy

Why it happens: Poor planning, burnout, distractions
Solution:

- Time-block 2 "power hours" per week just for your dream
- Remove one non-essential task from your schedule

Best Practice: Use the **Priority Matrix Chart**

Urgent & Important	Not Urgent but Important
Deadlines, emergencies	Long-term goals, skill-building
Delegate or Eliminate	Schedule for later

Concern #4: Financial Limitations

Why it happens: Overspending, lack of planning, fear of risk

Solution:

- Track your expenses and reallocate just **$50/week** toward your dream
- Start **small offers** (digital downloads, services)

Benchmark: Revenue Reinvestment Tracker

Income This Month	Reinvested	Spent	Saved
$500	$100 into business	$300	$100

Concern #5: Negative Mindset / Self-Doubt

Why it happens: Internal narratives, unsupportive environments
Solution: Create your **Power Statement**
"I am a creator. I bring ideas to life. I am valuable and unstoppable."

Affirmation Ritual:

- Say your power statement **every morning**
- Create a vision board for your goal

Concern #6: Poor Money Habits or No Structure

Why it happens: Emotional spending, no system
Solution:

- Use **automation** (savings, investments)
- Apply the **70-20-10 rule:**
    - 70% of expenses
    - 20% reinvest in business
    - 10% saving/investing

Concern #7: Lack of Accountability

Why it happens: Isolation, no feedback loop
Solution:

- Join a community or mastermind
- Find a **success partner**

Task:

Write down two people who could support your journey. Text or email them now.

Concern #8: Lack of Business Knowledge

Why it happens: Overwhelm, no roadmap

Solution:

- Start with one learning module at a time
- Take **micro-actions** as you learn

Weekly Learning Schedule:

Week	Focus	Resource
Week 1	Build a product idea	Workbook Ch.1
Week 2	Understand your market	Masterclass Ch.2
Week 3	Launch your offer	Ch.4 + Revenue System

PROGRESS TRACKER

Week	Key Goal	Done (✅)	Notes
1	Wrote down 3 product ideas		Feeling creative
2	Started learning Canva		Need more time
3	Sent an offer to 5 friends		Waiting on feedback

25 Practical Strategies to Activate "What's in Your Hands Today"

From the book: *Creativity Is Currency*

1. Identify Your Current Skills

Make a list of all your existing talents — what you do well, both naturally and through learned experience.

---

2. Audit Your Resources

Take stock of your available tools: time, relationships, devices, software, knowledge, etc.

---

3. Write Down Your Story

Your journey is valuable. Start documenting your past experiences, trials, and lessons. There's a message in your mess.

4. Choose One Area of Focus

Don't try to do everything at once. Select ONE idea or direction to develop first.

5. Define a Problem You Can Solve

What problem are people struggling with that your hands (skills/resources) can help solve?

6. Turn Your Passion Into a Product

Think about what lights you up — then ask, "Can this be turned into a service, product, or platform?"

7. Build a Simple MVP (Minimum Viable Product)

Create a basic version of your product or service. Focus on functionality, not perfection.

---

8. Use Free Tools to Start

Start with free resources: Canva for design, Google Docs for writing, Mailchimp for email lists, etc.

---

9. Host a Small Group or Live Q&A

Gather a few friends or connections to test your idea and get live feedback.

---

10. Set a 30-Day Action Plan

What can you accomplish in the next 30 days? Make a short, realistic action plan.

---

11. Record Your Knowledge

Start a blog, podcast, or video series sharing what you already know — your hands already hold wisdom.

---

12. Launch a Pre-Order or Pre-Sale

You don't need a finished product to sell it. Create interest and collect early buyers.

---

13. Build a Personal Brand

Start positioning yourself online with a professional bio, profile, and consistent messaging.

14. Build a Simple Email List

Utilize free platforms to collect emails and expand your community from the outset.

15. Ask for Testimonials

Even if you've only helped friends or family, ask them to write about how your "gift" helped them.

16. Read 1 Book Per Month to Grow

Start a reading routine that stretches your vision and sharpens your execution.

17. Create a Social Media Series

Educate your audience with what you know — 5 to 7 post series around one key idea.

18. Partner with Someone Who Compliments You

You don't need all the answers. Collaboration expands your capacity.

19. Offer a Beta Program

Offer a discounted version of your service to initial customers in exchange for their feedback.

20. Choose Progress Over Perfection

Focus on showing up and growing, not waiting for the perfect moment to launch.

21. Keep a Journal of Creative Thoughts

Write down all inspired ideas — many of them can be refined and developed over time.

---

22. Share Your Journey Publicly

Let people see your progress. It builds credibility and attracts supporters.

---

23. Measure One Key Metric Weekly

Set a measurable goal, such as increasing followers, email subscribers, or booking calls.

---

24. Celebrate Small Wins

Every step counts. Gratitude and acknowledgment fuel creative momentum.

---

25. Remind Yourself Daily: "I Have Enough to Begin"

Make this your mantra. Your hands are not empty — they are equipped.

Challenge:

Complete **"What's in My Hands"**:

- Skills audit
- Resources audit
- Passion inventory
- Problem they're passionate about solving
- One action to take THIS WEEK

You are not behind. You are being built.

Every obstacle you face has a solution, and this workbook helps you unlock it. Commit to this journey, and your reality will shift step by step. You are the creator. Your vision is valid. And your time is now.

Chapter Two

Wisdom Tracker: The Path to Purposeful Decisions

"Wisdom is the bridge between clarity and courage. When you know better, you do better—with purpose."

PART ONE: The Wisdom–Vision Connection

"Without vision, people perish. Without wisdom, they drift."

Reflection Prompt:

1. What vision are you currently pursuing in your life or business?
2. What specific decisions must be made to move that vision forward?
3. What type of wisdom do you need to make those decisions confidently?

Activity: Vision Alignment Check

Vision Area	Current Focus	Required Wisdom	Next Best Step
Personal Growth			
Financial Goals			
Relationships			

Vision Area	Current Focus	Required Wisdom	Next Best Step
Business/Career			

Activate Wisdom in Your Daily Life & Business Decisions

Theme: "Wise decisions today build unstoppable legacies tomorrow."

PART TWO: Daily Wisdom Practice

Mood Check-in:

Morning Reflection Prompt (Choose one to reflect on or journal briefly):

- What decision do I need wisdom for today?
- Where am I currently lacking clarity or direction?
- How can I show up with intention and wisdom in my actions today?

PART THREE: Decision-Making Checklist

Use this section before making key business or life decisions.

Check each box before moving forward.

Questions to Ask:

Does this align with my values and long-term goals?
Have I sought counsel or reflection before making a decision?
What are the short-term vs. long-term consequences?
Am I being reactive or intentional?
Will this decision add value to me or others?

PART FOUR: Daily Wisdom Score

Rate yourself from 1–5 on the following areas:

I paused and thought before responding.
I made a thoughtful decision today.
I aligned my actions with my values.
I learned something new that grew my mindset.
I communicated wisely and clearly with others.

Daily Wisdom Score: _______ / 25

PART FIVE: Weekly Wisdom Reflection

(Complete every 7 days)

This Week's Wisest Decision:

A Mistake I Learned From:

What I Need to Do Differently Next Week:

One Area I Need to Seek Counsel On:

Top 3 Insights From the Week:

1. ____

2. ____

3. ____

BONUS: Wisdom Growth Chart (Track Weekly Scores)

Week #	Daily Avg Score	Insight Summary
Week 1		
Week 2		
Week 3		
Week 4		

Affirmation

"I am guided by clarity, strengthened by purpose, and led by wisdom. My decisions reflect who I am becoming."

Wisdom Deficit Detector

Sometimes we're not lacking motivation; we're lacking **wise guidance**. Let's uncover what's lacking.

Circle the challenges you've faced recently:

- ☐ Confusion when choosing between two good options
- ☐ Regret from rushed decisions
- ☐ Misalignment with long-term goals
- ☐ Emotional decisions over strategic ones
- ☐ Lack of counsel or mentors
- ☐ Repeating the same mistakes

Prompt:

What lessons have you *refused to learn* that keep repeating themselves?

Action Step:

Write one decision you've made recently. Identify what wisdom could've improved that outcome.

Daily Wisdom Practice

"Wisdom isn't a lightning bolt—it's a discipline."

Activity: 7-Day Wisdom Builder

Day	Situation Needing Wisdom	Action Taken	What Did You Learn?	Who Did You Seek Counsel From?
1.				

Day	Situation Needing Wisdom	Action Taken	What Did You Learn?	Who Did You Seek Counsel From?
2.				
3.				
4.				
5.				
6.				
7.				

End-of-week reflection:

- What wisdom habits can I now begin to apply daily?
- What do I now see more clearly?

Wisdom + Vision = Legacy

"Every decision you make is either building or breaking your legacy."

Legacy Prompt:

- What kind of leader, creator, or legacy builder do you want to become?
- What decisions today reflect the person you are becoming tomorrow?

Chart: Wise Decision-Making Model

[VISION] → [Seek Understanding] → [Gain Counsel] → [Make Aligned Decision] → [Reflect & Refine]

---

25 Key Strategies to Create, Build, and Prosper with Wisdom

FOUNDATIONAL WISDOM STRATEGIES

1. **Pause Before Acting**
   Develop the habit of slowing down your decision-making process. Wisdom thrives in reflection, not in haste.
2. **Seek Counsel Early**
   Before launching or pivoting, consider seeking guidance from mentors, professionals, or spiritual leaders to inform your decision.
3. **Define Core Values**
   Make every business and creative decision flow from values that guide your life (e.g., integrity, excellence, service).
4. **Embrace Delayed Gratification**
   Choose a long-term reward over a short-term impulse. Wisdom always favors sustainable growth.

5. **Take Inventory of Experience**
   Review your wins and losses—your past teaches valuable lessons you can apply to future decisions.

CREATIVE WISDOM IN ACTION

6. **Test Small Before Scaling Big**
   Pilot your product or idea in a small market. Use feedback to refine your product before launching it fully.
7. **Ask: "Is This Idea Helpful?"**
   Filter ideas through usefulness, not just profit. If it helps others, it has lasting value.
8. **Learn from Other People's Mistakes**
   Wisdom doesn't just come from experience—it also comes from observation.
9. **Create Systems, Not Just Sparks**
   Don't just have great ideas—build systems to support and sustain those ideas.
10. **Honor the Seed Stage**
    Don't rush past the early messy stages of development. Wisdom says, "Build your roots before your branches."

FINANCIAL WISDOM STRATEGIES

11. **Separate Emotion from Money Decisions**
    Don't buy, invest, or spend based solely on hype or emotion—evaluate with clarity.
12. **Live Beneath Your Means While You Grow**
    Don't upgrade your lifestyle faster than your cash flow can support.
13. **Set Up an Emergency Business Fund**
    Wisdom plans for disruption—always have a cushion.
14. **Track ROI on Time and Money**
    Measure the tasks that yield the best return on investment. If it doesn't grow your vision, reevaluate.
15. **Build Multiple Revenue Streams Over Time**
    Don't put all your eggs in one creative basket. Let wisdom diversify your income.

RELATIONAL & LEADERSHIP WISDOM

16. **Protect Your Peace While Pursuing Purpose**
    Say "no" to what distracts. Guard your mental and emotional health.
17. **Collaborate with Complementary Strengths**
    Don't do everything alone—partner with people who are strong where you're weak.
18. **Lead with Empathy, Not Ego**
    Wisdom builds bridges, not silos. See people, not just productivity.

19. **Teach What You're Learning**
    Reinforce your wisdom by sharing it with others—it multiplies your impact.
20. **Be a Problem-Solver, Not a Blame-Thrower**
    Every business will hit friction. Use wisdom to seek solutions, not scapegoats.

SPIRITUAL & INTERNAL ALIGNMENT STRATEGIES

21. **Pray or Meditate Before Big Decisions**
    Connect with your higher purpose before making significant choices.
22. **Listen to Your Inner Conviction**
    Wisdom often whispers. Trust the gentle voice of "right vs. right now."
23. **Embrace Correction Without Shame**
    Learn from feedback with humility. Growth requires pruning.
24. **Visualize the Outcome of Today's Choice**
    Wisdom asks: "If I do this now, what will it produce later?"
25. **Be Intentional About Legacy**
    Every decision leaves a footprint. Use wisdom to build something worth leaving behind.

Summary: How Wisdom Creates Prosperity

Wisdom isn't just about what you know. It's how you apply what you've learned—consistently, patiently, and purposefully. These 25 strategies help you actively choose the path of long-term success, rather than merely pursuing short-term gains.

Call-to-Action:

Don't move fast without direction. Move with purpose.

- Review this weekly.
- Surround yourself with wise counsel.
- Never separate **your vision from wisdom**; they are twins of greatness.

Chapter Three

Become The Person Blueprint

Daily Blueprint to Transform Your Identity and Step into Your Calling

"You must become the person before you can receive what was always meant for you." – David Toliver

PURPOSE OF THIS BLUEPRINT

This blueprint is your daily companion to support personal transformation. You are not just chasing wealth—you are becoming a person of clarity, consistency, and character. Use this blueprint to track:

- Your mindset shifts
- Daily aligned actions
- Identity habits
- Purposeful decisions

DAILY MINDSET RESET

Morning Mindset Questions	Your Reflections
What kind of person must I be today to receive what I desire?	
What beliefs do I need to strengthen or release?	
What is one powerful thought I will carry with me today?	

"Transformation begins with how you think. Change your thoughts, and you change your life."

IDENTITY ALIGNMENT TRACKER

Use this weekly to reinforce who you're becoming.

Day	Identity Declaration	Behavior to Match	Did You Follow Through? (Y/N)
Mon	I am a disciplined creator.	Spend 2 hours building my system.	
Tue	I am a powerful communicator.	Delivered value through my brand voice.	
Wed	I am a person of value.	Solved one meaningful problem today.	

Day	Identity Declaration	Behavior to Match	Did You Follow Through? (Y/N)
Thu	I am aligned with my purpose.	Revisited goals and acted accordingly.	
Fri	I am the person who receives.	Practiced abundance and self-worth.	

ACTION STEPS TO BECOME

- **Clarify Your "Why"**
  Write your reason for transformation in one sentence:

  "I want to become the person who..."

- **Establish Non-Negotiables**
  List three daily habits your future self practices:

1. ______________________________

2. ______________________________

3. ______________________________

- **Track Key Decisions**
  Each day, reflect: Did I make a decision today that aligns with who I'm becoming?

- **Daily Action Commitment**
  Use the table below to log actions that reinforce your identity:

Date	Action Taken	Identity Reinforced	Outcome

REINFORCEMENT RITUAL (5 Minutes Each Night)

- What did I *learn* today?
- What *aligned action* did I take?
- What will I do differently tomorrow?
- Did I act like the person I want to become?

"Becoming is a process. Winning begins when your habits match your vision."

WEEKLY ALIGNMENT CHECK-IN

Week	Wins & Progress	Misalignments	Adjustments

YOUR FUTURE YOU: VISION JOURNAL PROMPT

"Describe the person you have become six months from now."

- How do you think?
- How do you act?
- What's changed in your finances, habits, and daily life?

WHO YOU'RE BECOMING

Trait	Current Level (1-10)	Target	Notes
Discipline			
Integrity			
Creativity			
Leadership			
Execution			

VISUAL TRANSFORMATION FRAMEWORK: FROM STRUGGLING TO STRONG & SUCCESSFUL

DIAGRAM: "The Diamond Within the Square"

Imagine a **square divided into four quadrants**—each representing a central life/business pillar—with a **diamond in the center**. This diamond is *"You"*, the *creator, unlocking the wealth within.*

[MINDSET] | [IDENTITY]

YOU: The Creator

[ACTION] | [IMPACT]

Quadrant 1: Mindset – "What You Think Shapes What You Do"

- **Problem:** Most people operate from survival-mode thinking.
- **Transformation:** You shift to vision-driven thinking, fueled by wisdom, clarity, and purpose.

Tools:

- "Wisdom Compass" chart to weigh decisions
- "Thought Audit" (track fear vs. faith-based thoughts)
- "Belief Shifter" (replace limiting beliefs with powerful affirmations)

Quadrant 2: Identity – "Become Before You Receive"

- **Problem:** You may feel unqualified, unseen, or unsure.
- **Transformation:** You begin *to own your creativity, positioning yourself as a problem-solver and value creator.*

Tools:

- "I AM" identity-builder page (Craft who you are becoming)
- "Essence Mirror Exercise" (How others experience your creativity)
- Role Model Mapping (Learn from those you aspire to emulate)

Quadrant 3: Action – "Create the Work Only You Can Do"

- **Problem:** You hesitate, waiting for permission or perfection.
- **Transformation:** You start producing—building offers, writing the first line, and recording the first pitch.

Tools:

- "What's in Your Hands?" Inventory
- Idea to Offer Builder (Step-by-step system from idea → value)
- 7-Day Momentum Map (1 major task per day to activate your ideas)

Quadrant 4: Impact – "Turn Value Into Influence"

- **Problem:** Creators struggle to share or monetize their work.

- **Transformation:** You begin telling your story, connecting with your audience, and delivering results worth paying for.

Tools:

- Brand Message Blueprint
- "Who Needs What I Have?"
- Influence Map (Chart how your gift spreads into the marketplace)

The Central Diamond: YOU – The Creator

You are not just someone with ideas, you are the one who turns them into impact and income.

The more you activate each quadrant:

- The sharper your identity becomes.
- The stronger your actions become.
- The greater your impact becomes.

VISUALS & ILLUSTRATIONS TO USE

Climb the Mountain –Ascending from "Stuck" → "Starter" → "Strategist" → "Success"

Before vs. After Mindset Table – Contrast scarcity with abundance, confusion with clarity

Vision Poster Template – Help you draw what success looks like

Roadmap Timeline – From Day 1 → 90 Days of Implementation

Wheel of Identity – Break down key roles (Leader, Creator, Communicator, Steward)

BUILDING THE PERSON YOU MUST BECOME

25 Strategies to Create, Build, and Prosper

1. Own Your Identity

Claim who you are as a creative and visionary. Define your purpose and reaffirm your right to build and create.

2. Reprogram Your Mindset

Remove scarcity thinking. Replace "I can't" with "I will." Challenge fear with intentional belief in abundance.

3. Set a Clear Vision

Define what success looks like for you. Write a vivid description of your future self—emotionally, spiritually, and financially.

4. Create Morning Mastery

Start each day with reflection, gratitude, goal setting, and creativity. Winners build from within first.

5. Journal Your Transformation

Track mindset shifts, wins, lessons, and setbacks. Review regularly to see how far you've come.

6. Speak the Language of the Future

Use affirmations and power statements to train your brain to expect what you want, not what you fear.

7. Develop Self-Discipline

Master your daily habits. Greatness is not about talent, it's about what you do when no one is watching.

8. Craft a Personal Brand Statement

Write one sentence that defines your value to the world. This becomes your guide for how you show up.

9. Identify Your Creative Strengths

Audit your natural talents. What do people always come to you for? This is where your genius lives.

10. Build an Idea Vault

Start documenting every idea, insight, concept, or invention that comes to mind. Your next big breakthrough might already be within you.

11. Learn the Art of Focus

Decide on one idea to build. Give it all your focus. Multitasking delays mastery.

12. Study the Wealthy

Discover the habits, mindset, and disciplines of individuals who have achieved financial independence through creativity.

13. Create Value Daily

Ask: "How can I solve a problem today?" Every act of service or creativity increases your market value.

14. Build a Creator Circle

Surround yourself with people who are building, creating, and prospering. Mindsets are contagious.

15. Invest in Your Skill Set

Take a course, hire a coach, read a book. Skill-building increases confidence and income.

16. Develop a Feedback Loop

Invite honest feedback from mentors or peers. Use it to refine your product, process, or pitch.

17. Take Bold, Imperfect Action

Perfection is the enemy of progress. Build while you learn. Adjust as you grow.

18. Visualize Daily

Close your eyes and imagine your life after success. Feel it in your body. Act from that version of you today.

19. Practice Decision-Making Power

Decide quickly. Wealth builders don't waver. They trust themselves and adjust as needed.

20. Give Before You Receive

Offer value freely—insights, help, inspiration. Giving makes you magnetic to opportunity.

21. Establish Creator Rituals

Protect time daily to build your business, refine your idea, or promote your brand. Rituals shape results.

22. Monetize What You Know

Create a product, service, or workshop from your story, insight, or skill. You already have value inside you.

23. Celebrate Small Wins

Every victory is evidence that you are becoming. Track and celebrate progress.

24. Commit to a Long-Term Vision

Don't build for fast cash. Build for legacy. Your vision must outlive the temporary.

25. Walk in Faith

Believe in what you can't yet see. Move as if it's already yours. Create from the Creator within.

Final Thought:

You don't become wealthy when the money arrives; you become wealthy when you change how you think, believe, speak, and create. These 25 strategies aren't just actions; they are the blueprints for **becoming the person who is ready to receive and multiply abundance**.

Are you ready to become that person?

Let's build.

CALL TO ACTION

"The person you're becoming is waiting for your permission."

Becoming the person you want to be is about shifting your beliefs, upgrading your habits, and aligning with your future. Don't just read this chapter—track it, live it, become it. You are the receiver now.

YOU: The Creator

Chapter Four

Chapter Four: Build Your Financial Wisdom

Chapter Theme:
Seeking Godly and professional financial counsel is critical to building, managing, and preserving wealth.

Section 1: Self-Assessment — Where Are You Today?

Rate yourself on the scale of 1–5 (1 = strongly disagree, 5 = strongly agree):

Statement	Rating (1–5)
I regularly seek God's wisdom before making financial decisions.	☐
I have a financial advisor or coach I trust.	☐
I understand how my money is working for me today.	☐
I have a long-term wealth-building plan in place.	☐
I've educated myself on taxes, insurance, and investing.	☐

Total Score: _____ / 25

Reflection: What does your score reveal about your financial wisdom?

Section 2: Identify the Gaps

Check any area(s) where you feel unsure, unprepared, or uneducated:

- Understanding taxes and how they impact my revenue
- Investing: stock market, real estate, crypto, or others
- Estate planning (will, trust, legacy)
- Insurance protection (life, liability, business)
- Hiring or evaluating a financial advisor
- Creating generational wealth strategies
- Biblical and spiritual principles of stewardship

What's one area that, if mastered, would change everything for your financial future?

Section 3: Your Financial Wisdom Growth Plan

Based on Chapter Four's teachings, choose your next steps:

Strategy	Action Step	Deadline	Accountability
Seek God's guidance in finances.	Start a 7-day prayer & journal challenge	[Date]	[Person or Reminder]
Connect with a financial advisor.	Research 3 local or virtual advisors	[Date]	[Person or Reminder]
Improve money education	Read one book or take one course on investing	[Date]	[Person or Reminder]
Build family financial discussions.	Host a family "wealth night"	[Date]	[Person or Reminder]

Visual: Financial Wisdom Impact Chart

Wisdom Applied	Result	Long-Term Benefit
Strategic Counsel	Make informed decisions	Reduced risk & increased ROI
Faith-Driven Financial Planning	Peace & purpose	Aligned values with vision
Ongoing Financial Education	Empowered mindset	Generational impact

Reflection Prompt

"What kind of financial legacy do I want to leave behind?"

Write your answer below. Speak from your heart.

Challenge:

Write your "Financial Wisdom Declaration."

"I am committed to seeking godly and wise financial counsel. I will grow, protect, and multiply my resources with clarity, purpose, and intention. My money will serve a purpose beyond me — for my family, community, and legacy."

Customize your version below:

"I am committed to..."

What Is Financial Wisdom—And Why It Matters

Financial wisdom is not just knowing how money works—it's understanding why it matters, how to use it for a purpose, and how to align your financial life with your greater mission. It's about seeing money as a **means, not an end in itself**.

VISUAL FRAMEWORK: "The Financial Wisdom Diamond"

Here's a visual model we'll use to deepen the learning:

[Long-Term Vision] [Daily Habits]

◄————————◆————————► YOU: The Creator

[Character & Values] [Practical Knowledge]

Center Diamond (◆): YOU, the Creator

You are at the center, activating each point of financial wisdom through action and reflection.

DEEPER WISDOM PRINCIPLES

Here are five high-level principles that will elevate your financial mindset:

1. Wisdom Makes You Pause Before You Purchase

Instead of reacting emotionally, wisdom asks:

"Is this aligned with my future or just my momentary feelings?"

Reflection Prompt:
Write down your last three purchases. Which of them were rooted in wisdom? What drove each one?

---

2. Wisdom Learns from Mistakes—Not Just Success

A wise person doesn't avoid failure—they learn from it fast and adjust quickly.

Journal Prompt:
What's one past financial mistake you can use as a teaching point today? What lesson did it teach?

---

3. Wisdom Knows the Cost of Delay

Putting off investing, learning, or building your skills is one of the costliest decisions you can make. Wisdom creates a sense of urgency, not panic, but purpose.

Benchmark Chart:

Delay (in years)	Lost Potential Growth (based on $5k/year, 8%)
0 years	$375,000+
5 years	$250,000+
10 years	$150,000+

Lesson: Start now.

---

4. Wisdom Builds Financial Boundaries

This includes savings, spending limits, giving intentionally, and investing wisely.

Diagram:
"4 Walls of Financial Boundaries"

1. **Spending Cap** – Limits waste.
2. **Saving Discipline** – Builds your cushion.
3. **Giving Target–Fuels** purpose.
4. **Investing Plan** – Grows your future.

---

5. Wisdom Seeks Counsel Before Crisis

Financial wisdom is humble. It doesn't assume it knows everything. It asks, listens, and learns.

Action Step:

Name 2-3 people (or professionals) who can mentor or advise you financially.

BENCHMARK: Where Am I Now?

Create your financial wisdom score using the scale below.

Financial Wisdom Area	Score 1-5	Notes
I have a long-term money vision.		
I make value-based spending decisions.		
I learn from financial mistakes.		
I use money to solve problems for others.		
I actively seek wise counsel.		
I have a giving plan.		
I've started investing consistently.		

TOTAL SCORE: ______ / 35

Interpretation:

- 0–15: It's time to start building your financial wisdom.
- 16–25: You're learning! Keep growing.
- 26–35: You're walking in wisdom—now teach others.

CALL TO ACTION: What You Must Do Now

1. **Start tracking every financial decision this week.**
    - What was the motive? Emotion or wisdom?
2. **Choose one area to strengthen: vision, values, or habits.**
3. "I will no longer allow confusion, fear, or delay to rule my financial life. I walk in wisdom. I build wealth with purpose. I use money to fulfill my calling."

Center Diamond (◆): YOU, the Creator

You are at the center, activating each point of financial wisdom through action and reflection.

DEEPER WISDOM PRINCIPLES

Here are five high-level principles that will elevate your financial mindset:

1. Wisdom Makes You Pause Before You Purchase

Instead of reacting emotionally, wisdom asks:

"Is this aligned with my future or just my momentary feelings?"

Reflection Prompt:
Write down your last three purchases. Which of them were rooted in wisdom? What drove each one?

2. Wisdom Learns from Mistakes—Not Just Success

A wise person doesn't avoid failure—they learn from it fast and adjust quickly.

Journal Prompt:
What's one past financial mistake you can use as a teaching point today? What lesson did it teach?

3. Wisdom Knows the Cost of Delay

Putting off investing, learning, or building your skills is one of the costliest decisions you can make. Wisdom creates a sense of urgency, not panic, but purpose.

Benchmark Chart:

Delay (in years)	Lost Potential Growth (based on $5k/year, 8%)
0 years	$375,000+
5 years	$250,000+
10 years	$150,000+

Lesson: Start now.

4. Wisdom Builds Financial Boundaries

This includes savings, spending limits, giving intentionally, and investing wisely.

Diagram:
"4 Walls of Financial Boundaries"

1. **Spending Cap** – Limits waste.
2. **Saving Discipline** – Builds your cushion.
3. **Giving Target–Fuels** purpose.
4. **Investing Plan** – Grows your future.

---

5. Wisdom Seeks Counsel Before Crisis

Financial wisdom is humble. It doesn't assume it knows everything. It asks, listens, and learns.

Action Step:
Name 2-3 people (or professionals) who can mentor or advise you financially.

Where Am I Now?

Create your financial wisdom score using the scale below.

Financial Wisdom Area	Score 1-5	Notes
I have a long-term money vision.		
I make values-based spending decisions.		
I learn from financial mistakes.		
I use money to solve problems for others.		
I actively seek wise counsel.		
I have a giving plan.		
I've started investing consistently.		

TOTAL SCORE: ______ / 35

Interpretation:

- 0–15: It's time to start building your financial wisdom.
- 16–25: You're learning! Keep growing.
- 26–35: You're walking in wisdom—now teach others.

What Kind of Advisor Do You Need?

25 Key Strategies to Create, Build & Prosper With Your Idea

IDENTIFYING THE RIGHT ADVISORS

1. **Define Your Vision First**
   Get clear on your mission, your product/service, and what outcome you're pursuing. This helps identify *who* you need to support.
2. **Identify the Gaps in Your Knowledge**
   Do you lack financial expertise? Legal guidance? Marketing strategy? Pinpoint those gaps.
3. **Create an Advisor Map**
   Draw out the four areas of your business (Idea, Operations, Growth, Legal/Finance) and place the advisor roles you need in each quadrant.
4. **Seek Experience Over Theory**
   Look for advisors who've *done* what you're trying to do, not just those who talk about it.
5. **Interview Potential Advisors**
   Ask questions about how they've helped others like you. Don't be afraid to qualify them.

BUILDING AN ADVISORY NETWORK

6. **Find a Financial Advisor**
   Someone who can help you build wealth and manage cash flow effectively.

7. **Add a Legal Advisor**
   To protect your business and ensure you're compliant (trademarks, contracts, IP).
8. **Hire a Business Mentor or Coach**
   Someone who has walked your path can see around corners and guide your growth.
9. **Tap Into a Marketing/Branding Strategist**
   Find someone who understands storytelling, customer targeting, and brand building.
10. **Find a Tech or Systems Advisor**
   They'll help you scale your operations efficiently using tools and platforms.

MAXIMIZING ADVISOR VALUE

11. **Set Expectations Early**
   Clarify communication, frequency, compensation (if applicable), and goals.
12. **Create a Monthly Advisor Review Plan**
   Dedicate 1 day a month to meet with, reflect on, and implement advisor insights.
13. **Track ROI From Each Advisor**
   What results are they helping you get? Is it revenue, clarity, systems, or exposure?
14. **Bring Advisors Into Strategy, Not Just Problems**
   Ask them to help co-design the future, not just fix the present.

15. **Pay for Quality When Possible**
    A cheap advisor could end up costing you more in the long run. Invest wisely.

PROSPERING WITH GUIDANCE

16. **Apply Their Wisdom, Don't Just Hear It**
    Success comes from *action*. Execute their advice promptly and thoroughly.
17. **Build Relationships, Not Just Transactions**
    Treat advisors like partners. Create mutual value and show appreciation.
18. **Create an "Inner Circle" of Top Advisors**
    3–5 people you trust deeply who understand your mission and keep you aligned.
19. **Document Your Learnings**
    Keep a journal or digital log of the advice given, actions taken, and outcomes.
20. **Share Your Progress**
    Advisors invest in your vision. Update them with wins. They'll want to keep helping.

GROWING BEYOND ADVICE

21. **Graduate From Mentorship to Mastery**
Once you've learned enough, begin mentoring others in your space.
22. **Host Roundtables or Strategy Sessions**
Get multiple advisors together to help you problem-solve collaboratively.
23. **Build an Advisory Board for Your Business**
Formalize their role to provide you with strategic insights over the long term.
24. **Never Be the Smartest in the Room**
Surround yourself with brilliance so you're always learning and expanding.
25. **Honor the Journey**
Remember: advisors don't *do the work* for you—they *guide* the work. Be coachable, courageous, and committed.

BONUS TOOL: Advisor Alignment Chart

Advisor Type	Expertise Area	Why You Need Them	Frequency of Check-in
Financial Advisor	Cash flow, planning	Helps structure wealth, reduce waste	Monthly
Legal Advisor	Compliance, contracts	Protects assets, avoids legal risks	Quarterly

Advisor Type	Expertise Area	Why You Need Them	Frequency of Check-in
Business Coach	Growth strategy	Provides accountability and focus	Weekly/Biweekly
Branding Specialist	Messaging, marketing	Builds visibility and customer trust	Monthly
Systems/Tech Mentor	Automation, scaling	Helps simplify operations for growth	Monthly

CALL TO ACTION: What You Must Do Now

1. Do you currently have these in place? Living vs. Testamentary Trust and Revocable vs Irrevocable Trust?
2. **Start tracking every financial decision this week.**
3. What was the motive? Emotion or wisdom?
4. **Choose one area to strengthen: vision, values, or habits.**
5. "I will no longer allow confusion, fear, or delay to rule my financial life. I walk in wisdom. I build wealth with purpose. I use money to fulfill my calling."

Chapter Five

Legacy Builder Blueprint

Building Generational Wealth with Purpose, Vision, and Strategy

---

Section 1: Your Legacy Vision

Define your long-term vision that will outlive you and impact future generations.

1. What legacy do you want to leave for your children and grandchildren?

☐ Personal Values
☐ Financial Stability
☐ Education & Wisdom
☐ Entrepreneurial Opportunity
☐ Faith & Character
☐ Other: ___________________________

Write your legacy vision in 1–2 bold sentences:

"I want my legacy to..."

Section 2: Your Family Core Values

Establish the values your family will be known for.

Core Value	Description & Family Meaning	How It's Practiced Today
Example: Integrity	We tell the truth even when it's hard.	Family meetings, honesty talks

Section 3: Wealth Transfer Plan

Craft a multi-generational financial strategy.
(Use this to create your will, trust, and asset protection plan.)

1. Do you currently have these in place?

☐ Will

☐ Living Trust

☐ Life Insurance

☐ Financial Power of Attorney

☐ Beneficiary Forms Updated

2. Who are your future wealth stewards (trustees, business successors, etc.)?

- Name: ______________________ | Role: __________________
- Name: ______________________ | Role:__________________

3. What assets will you pass down?

☐ Property

☐ Investments

☐ Intellectual Property (e.g., book, business, brand)

☐ Business Equity

☐ Real Estate Portfolio

☐ Other: ______________________

Section 4: Family Wealth Blueprint Chart

Your Legacy Plan Over Time

Create a tiered plan for today, 5 years, 10 years, and beyond.

Period	Legacy Milestones	Notes/Benchmarks
0–2 Years	Build trust, create an estate plan	Finalize legal structure
3–5 Years	Teach financial literacy to the family	Include next gen in money talks
6–10 Years	Transfer partial assets/businesses	Mentor heirs, establish systems
11+ Years	Legacy execution + review	Document lessons learned

Section 5: Family Financial Education

"Knowledge passed down becomes wealth sustained."

What wealth-building knowledge do you want your family to master?

☐ Budgeting

☐ Investing

☐ Business Ownership

☐ Property Management

☐ Philanthropy & Giving

☐ Other: ______________________

Resources You Will Share with Your Family:

Books, courses, family council meetings, real estate mentorships, etc.

Section 6: Family Governance Structure

Ensure your family legacy has order and longevity.

Governance Element	Who's Involved?	Frequency or Notes
Family Wealth Meetings	______________________	Quarterly

Governance Element	Who's Involved?	Frequency or Notes
Decision-Making Board	______________	Annual Review
Legacy Communication	______________	Legacy Letter / Time Capsule
Giving/Charity Strategy	______________	Tithes, scholarships, foundations

Final Reflection:

What one action will you take this week to begin your legacy plan?

____

Write your intention here:

"My legacy begins with..."

Why Legacy Building Is Vital to Your Family

1. Because Your Family Deserves More Than Just Memories

You are not just living for today — you are laying the foundation for generations yet unborn. Your legacy is the blueprint your family will follow when your voice is no longer there. Will they inherit a legacy of survival or strategy, opportunity, and empowerment?

You get to decide.

When you build a legacy, you ensure your children and their children don't have to start from scratch. You create continuity — a bridge from your effort to their advantage.

"Legacy is not leaving something for people. It's leaving something in people."

---

2. Legacy Gives Your Life Purpose and Direction

A true legacy is not accidental — it's intentional.

It's what gets you out of bed each morning. It drives your decisions, your sacrifices, and your discipline. It forces you to think beyond instant gratification. It demands that you not only accumulate wealth, but also preserve and protect it.

When you think about legacy, you think:

- "How will my children remember me?"
- "What will my name mean when I'm no longer here?"
- "What story will my life tell?"

And those questions shape your life into something focused, fruitful, and fulfilling.

What Legacy Building Truly Looks Like

Let's move past theory. Here's what it **looks like** when you start building a legacy:

1. Financial Infrastructure

- Set up a trust or **will**
- Ensure proper **insurance coverage** (life, health, long-term care)
- Create passive income systems (real estate, royalties, automated business models)
- Assign financial mentors or advisors to your family members

2. Education & Knowledge Transfer

- Teach your family about money — not just how to spend it, but how to multiply it
- Pass on your **wealth-building systems** and the **story behind them**
- Leave **written lessons** and **recorded insights** (letters, videos, etc.)

- Encourage critical thinking, faith, and entrepreneurial spirit

3. Values & Identity

- Clarify the core values of your household (e.g., faith, integrity, creativity, service)
- Design a family mission statement
- Schedule legacy-building days: vision casting, skill-building, family finance reviews
- Celebrate "legacy moments" — new jobs, new businesses, land purchases, and breakthroughs

4. Sustainability Systems

- Create structures for accountability (a family board, regular check-ins)
- Reinvest in family business or family causes
- Build in charitable giving and community impact
- Protect assets through **diversification**, **legal structures**, and **financial literacy**

The Endless Benefits of Legacy

Legacy protects your name.
It opens doors you'll never walk through.
It puts your family in rooms they couldn't otherwise access.
It creates spiritual and emotional safety.
It gives your children the gift of choices.

A strong legacy says, *"I was here. And I made sure you could go further than I ever could."*

---

25 Practical Strategies to Apply the Generational Wealth Assessment

1. Identify Your Wealth-Building Strength

Assessment Strategy: Identify your top creative or business strengths through self-assessment and feedback.
Application: Double down on this strength and use it to lead your generational wealth plan.

---

2. Establish Your Legacy Vision

Assessment Strategy: Write a personal wealth mission and vision statement.
Application: Let this vision shape your business, brand, and financial decisions.

---

3. Inventory Your Current Assets

Assessment Strategy: Track all your assets: knowledge, time, skills, property, tools, and networks.

Application: Leverage overlooked assets (like your creativity or relationships) to start building.

---

4. Audit Your Financial Mindset

Assessment Strategy: Utilize reflection prompts to uncover limiting beliefs surrounding money, wealth, and creativity.
Application: Replace scarcity thinking with abundance and growth mindsets.

---

5. Clarify Your Generational Why

Assessment Strategy: Identify your "why" for building generational wealth.
Application: Use this to power through doubt, setbacks, and fatigue.

---

6. Define Your Creative Business Model

Assessment Strategy: Select a revenue-generating model that aligns with your lifestyle and personal interests.
Application: Decide—are you selling knowledge, products, content, or services?

---

7. Launch a Micro-Offer

Assessment Strategy: Begin with a single, targeted offer that addresses a specific problem.
Application: Validate the offer quickly and scale based on feedback.

---

8. Set Legacy-Based Financial Goals

Assessment Strategy: Create short- and long-term goals rooted in legacy, not just luxury.
Application: Tie each goal to a desired outcome for future generations.

---

9. Set Up a Financial Dashboard

Assessment Strategy: Utilize a system to track income, expenses, and savings every week.
Application: Monitor cash flow and redirect funds to investments or education.

---

10. Choose Your Income Streams

Assessment Strategy: Choose at least three streams (ex, content, services, digital products).
Application: Build and layer them over time.

---

11. Commit to Daily Wealth Habits

Assessment Strategy: Identify habits that improve focus, strategy, and creativity.
Application: Commit to 30 minutes/day of wealth-generating activity.

---

12. Create a Knowledge Legacy

Assessment Strategy: List your expertise and how you'll document it (books, courses, videos).
Application: Turn your knowledge into valuable assets.

---

13. Use Family Wealth Meetings

Assessment Strategy: Host regular talks with your children, spouse, or family.
Application: Teach the next generation while building with them.

---

14. Develop a Trust or Will

Assessment Strategy: Ensure your intellectual and business assets are protected legally.
Application: Work with a financial advisor or estate planner.

---

15. Build Your Wealth Identity

Assessment Strategy: Answer the question: "Who are you as a wealth builder?"
Application: Embody that identity in actions and branding.

---

16. Create a Generational Wealth Binder

Assessment Strategy: Compile all your documents: business, life insurance, real estate, IP rights.
Application: Pass this binder on as a blueprint for your family.

---

17. Invest in Business Education

Assessment Strategy: Choose one skill to master each quarter (e.g., sales, marketing, leadership).
Application: Apply it immediately in your business.

---

18. Track Generational Impact Metrics

Assessment Strategy: Define success by impact, not just income.
Application: Measure how many lives you impact, not just dollars.

19. Create Intellectual Property

Assessment Strategy: Package your creativity into things you own (courses, frameworks, books).
Application: Protect and monetize your IP for future generations.

20. Establish a Giving Plan

Assessment Strategy: Define how you'll give back—time, money, wisdom.
Application: Integrate philanthropy into your wealth strategy.

21. Build a Creative Advisory Board

Assessment Strategy: Surround yourself with 3–5 advisors (legal, financial, branding, creative).
Application: Let them help protect and scale your wealth vision.

22. Automate Wealth Habits

Assessment Strategy: Systematize savings, investments, and donations.
Application: Use automation tools and financial apps.

23. Evaluate Your Legacy Quarterly

Assessment Strategy: Reflect on the progress of your business, mindset, and legacy.
Application: Adjust plans based on what's working—and what's not.

---

24. Teach What You Learn

Assessment Strategy: Share insights with mentees, youth, or your community.
Application: Create a culture of creativity + wealth around you.

---

25. Craft a Family Legacy Story

Assessment Strategy: Document your journey in a story format.
Application: Pass down wisdom, not just wealth, through generations.

Wealth Tracker Template:

- **Columns to Include:**
    - Revenue Stream Name
    - Monthly Income
    - Year-to-Date Total
    - System Used (Course, Book, Coaching, etc.)
    - Cost of Maintenance

- Passive or Active?
- Notes:

Word to You

You are not just building wealth.
You are writing your family's future.
You are breaking cycles.
You are building bridges.

What you start today may be why your great-grandchild doesn't have to beg, borrow, or break down to survive.

Start now. This is your moment. This is your mission.

Bonus: Legacy Accountability Partner

Who can you trust to hold you accountable to your legacy-building goals?
Name: ______________________________
Contact: _____________________________

Chapter Six

What Your Hand Findeth to Do, Do It with All Your Might

Subtitle: Ignite Commitment • Build Momentum • Take Full Ownership

Section 1: Decide to Take the Journey

"Whatever your hand finds to do, do it with all your might." — Ecclesiastes 9:10

Prompt:

☐ What decision do I need to commit to today fully?

☐ What has stopped me from going "all in" with my gifts or business idea?

☐ What does "doing it with all my might" look like in my daily routine?

Action Step:

Write a commitment statement you will declare each morning:

"Today I will ________ with all my might because I am called to create and contribute."

Section 2: Commitment Sparks Possibility

Commitment is the spark that ignites your potential. When you commit fully, the path begins to form beneath your feet.

Benchmark Assessment (Scale 1–10):

☐ My current level of commitment to my goals: ____/10
☐ My consistency in showing up with discipline: ____/10
☐ My belief in my ability to succeed: ____/10

Growth Insight:

If your numbers are under 7, what do you need to let go of or transform? What's one new behavior you can practice this week to boost your commitment?

Section 3: Build a Strong Mindset & Knowledge Base

A wealthy life begins with a transformed mind. What you believe determines what you pursue. What you learn determines what you earn.

Mindset Reflection:

☐ I believe I have what it takes to succeed.
☐ I am willing to unlearn and relearn.
☐ I surround myself with people who challenge and uplift me.

Knowledge Strategy:

Identify three new skills you must master to succeed:

1. ______________________________

2. ______________________________

3. ______________________________

What book, course, or mentor can help you develop these?

Section 4: Turn Work Ethic Into Wealth

Work ethic isn't just about hustle, but about intentional and *strategic action.*

Work Ethic Alignment Chart:

Task or Action	Impact Level	Time Invested	Is this aligned with my purpose? (Yes/No)

Next Step:

☐ Eliminate or delegate anything that isn't purpose-aligned.

☐ Double down on high-impact activities that move the needle forward.

Final Section: Visualize the Person Who Finishes Strong

☐ Draw or write a vivid description of who you are after you've completed this journey:
– What do you look like?
– What are you doing every day?
– How do people describe you?
– What do your results say about your effort?

"Whatever your hand finds to do, do it with all your might." – Ecclesiastes 9:10

Mindset Foundation: "Become the Person Who Can Handle the Reward"

Before success can manifest in your bank account, you must first embed it **in your belief system**.

The right-minded frame is not optional. It is everything. Your dream will stall if your vision is powerful, but your habits are inconsistent. This chapter brings you face to face with a life-changing truth:

You don't get what you want. You get what you're ready for.

Here's how to shape that readiness:

1. Anchor in Purpose

Know *why* you are doing the work. Without purpose, you will drift or burn out. Your purpose fuels your "might."

2. Adopt a Creator Mindset

You are not a consumer only. You were made to **create, build, and shape** your outcomes. You have a vision to manifest and problems to solve. Think like a producer.

3. Develop Mental Resilience

You will face adversity. The difference between the wealthy and the struggling is not talent — it's mental toughness. *Decide in advance not to quit.*

Topics to Build Something Great :
Focus:

1. The Power of Clear Intention

When you work with *clarity* and *focus*, your results multiply. Many people don't see progress because they scatter their energy across many projects.

Ask yourself:

- What am I building right now?
- What one action can I do *today* to move it forward?

---

2. Imagination + Communication = Income

You don't get paid for ideas. You get paid for:

- **Solving problems**
- **Sharing your solution**
- **Presenting it well**

That means your ability to **speak, teach, sell, and inspire others** is directly tied to your income.

"The more you can communicate the value you provide, the more wealth you attract."

Practice writing your idea, pitching your solution to someone, teaching your concept aloud, receiving feedback, and repeating the process.

---

3. Creating Systems, Not Just Working Hard

Hard work isn't the goal — **brilliant work that scales is**.

"If your income stops when you stop working, you're not building wealth — you're just busy."

Here's what to build instead:

- A digital product (eBook, online course)
- A subscription-based offer
- A coaching or service-based system
- A license or IP-based offer
- Real estate or passive income investments

Systems create freedom. Manual labor keeps you bound.

Benchmark: Wealth Readiness Scorecard

Use this to reflect on your current mindset and business development.

Category	Question	Score (1-5)
Purpose Clarity	Do I know why I'm building this business?	
Skill Set Strength	Have I mastered a specific, valuable skill?	
Communication Impact	Can I clearly explain my idea and why it matters?	
System Creation	Do I have repeatable systems that produce revenue?	

Category	Question	Score (1-5)
Execution Discipline	Am I working daily toward my goals with focus and consistency?	

Total Score:

- 20–25: You're ready to scale
- 15–19: You're building strong momentum
- 10–14: You need to sharpen your focus and daily action
- Below 10: It's time to commit fully and go all in

Action Plan: Building Your Might

1. Identify Your Current Opportunity

- What's already in your hand? (Skills, contacts, tools, knowledge)
- What can you offer *right now* that people would pay for?

2. Develop It With All Your Might

- Commit to 90 days of focused development.
- Track your progress daily.
- Share it publicly to build momentum and accountability.

3. Communicate Like a Leader

- Start small. Record a video. Post your idea. Ask for feedback.
- Build a habit of sharing your solution with confidence.

4. Build a Revenue System

- Turn your idea into a repeatable offer.
- Package your skills.
- Launch, measure, and improve.

---

25 Practical Daily Execution Strategies:

Create – Build – Prosper

CREATE: Fuel the Idea

These first steps spark creativity and refine the vision.

1. **Morning Mindset Reset**
    - Start each day by declaring your creative identity. Write down one empowering affirmation about your creative power.

2. **Idea Dump Session**
    - Spend 10–15 minutes daily writing every idea that comes to mind. No filter. This builds a habit of generating possibilities.

3. **Problem-Solving Prompt**
    - Ask: *"What pain or inconvenience in the world can my idea solve today?"*
4. **Customer Avatar Check-In**
    - Revisit who you're building for. Define one specific person who will benefit today.
5. **Micro-Vision Mapping**
    - Sketch your idea in one sentence, one image, and one transformation you want others to experience.

BUILD: Take Daily Action

This is about developing the structure, system, and solution.

6. **One Daily Action Rule**
    - Identify one task that must get done today to move your idea forward, no matter how small.
7. **Block Your Time**
    - Use time blocks (e.g., Power Hour) to separate creative building, administration, and marketing tasks.
8. **Prototype Progress**
    - Build a version of your offer. It can be as simple as a landing page, outline, or conversation with your audience.
9. **Test Before You Perfect**
    - Get feedback fast. Don't wait for it to be perfect — show your rough draft to someone you trust.

10. **Build in Public**

- Post one insight, challenge, or progress on social media to build accountability and connection.

11. **Value Story Creation**

- Craft a short story that shows how your idea solves a problem in someone's life.

12. **Create a Checklist**

- Break your product or service into deliverables and check off daily what's been done. Momentum matters.

13. **Ask 3 People**

- Ask three people every week: *"Would this be valuable to you? Why or why not?"*

14. **Document Daily Wins**

- Keep a win journal. It helps keep the creator's momentum alive.

PROSPER: Monetize with Meaning

These final strategies focus on receiving compensation, creating transformation, and building financial traction.

15. **Offer Clarity Formula**

- Each day, refine your pitch using: *"I help [who] do [what], so they can [why it matters]."*

16. **Value Stack Practice**

- Add one bonus, one new benefit, or one visual to improve the offer.

17. **Set a Daily Revenue Goal**

- Even if symbolic (e.g., $10), aim for consistent sales-focused action daily.

18. **Follow Up with Purpose**

- Create a "warm list" of people who've shown interest. Follow up weekly with encouragement, not pressure.

19. **Create One Offer a Week**

- One new downloadable coaching session or workshop offer — test what resonates.

20. **Price and Package Review**

- Review your pricing every week to ensure accuracy and competitiveness. Are you aligned with the value you deliver?

21. **Celebrate Every Sale**

- No matter the size, gratitude fuels prosperity. Write a thank-you note to the customer, even if it's a private one.

22. **Collect Stories**

- Ask clients: *"How did this help you?"* Build a results wall – even screenshots can be helpful.

23. **Optimize One Funnel Step**

- Review one piece of your funnel, such as your landing page, email, or lead magnet, and make one improvement.

24. **Track Your Numbers**

- Use a simple spreadsheet to log leads, conversations, and conversions daily.

25. **Share the Journey**

- Let your audience know what this idea means to YOU. People don't just buy products – they buy vision.

Suggested Tracking Tools:

- Daily Execution Map Journal
- Visual Progress Tracker (bar graph, milestones)

- Weekly Scorecard for:
    - Ideas Generated
    - Tasks Completed
    - People Engaged
    - Income Earned

Words of Encouragement:

You don't have to be perfect. You don't need a degree. You don't need permission.
What you *do* need is:
✓A made-up mind
✓A willingness to take imperfect action
✓A decision to finish what you start

The work you do now will have a lasting impact on your future.
Give it everything.
Build like your legacy depends on it — because it does.

You are not here to live an average life.
You are not here to keep your brilliance hidden.
You are here to **create**, to **solve**, and to **shine**.

Whatever your hand finds to do — do it boldly. Do it wisely. Do it with all your might.
Because what you do today is build your wealth tomorrow.

Chapter Six Wrap-Up Commitment

"I commit to showing up with boldness, resilience, and strategy. I will work with *all my might* to honor the gift in my hands, the vision in my heart, and the value I'm called to create."

☐ Signed: ______________________________

☐ Date: _________________________________

Chapter Seven: Legacy Giving Blueprint

"When you have enough, give enough where it counts."

WHAT IS LEGACY GIVING?

Legacy Giving is the intentional act of giving with purpose, beyond charity, beyond obligation. It is a personal and spiritual decision to use the wealth you've built to **change lives**, **uplift communities**, and **impact generations**. It's not just about giving money—it's about giving meaning.

WHY GIVE?

- **To honor the journey:** You've walked through hardship, earned your success, and now stand on higher ground. Giving helps you reach back.
- **To create impact:** Your wealth can solve real problems—educate children, feed families, and fund missions or movements that change the world.
- **To leave a legacy:** What you build can live far beyond your years. Legacy giving ensures your values, dreams, and influence live on.

THE PURPOSE OF GIVING

1. **To Restore Hope** – Giving shows people they are seen, valued, and not forgotten.
2. **To Build Equity** – Your resources can close gaps and open doors for others.
3. **To Fulfill Purpose** – Giving activates your calling—it's not just about success, it's about significance.
4. **To Establish Kingdom Influence** – Giving reflects God's heart through your hands.

YOUR LEGACY GIVING PLAN

1. Identify Your "Why"

Ask yourself:

- Who do I want to help?
- What causes are close to my heart?
- What change do I want to see in the world where I live?

Legacy lives in clarity. Your "why" is your compass.

---

2. Choose Your "What"

What assets will you give?

✓Time
✓Talent
✓Money
✓Support local businesses
✓Food security
✓Charitable donations
✓Access (introductions, mentorship)

You don't need millions to be generous. Give what you have, with what you value.

---

3. Establish a Giving Rhythm

Create a system of generosity:

Frequency	Example
Weekly	Give to local families, fund meals, and sponsor students.
Monthly	Tithe, support missions, fund nonprofits
Quarterly	Host free coaching sessions, support startups
Annually	Fund scholarships, donate business profits, and establish legacy gifts.

Consistency beats one-time giving.

---

4. Define Your Impact Goals

Use this simple table to identify where you want to give and what results you hope to achieve.

Impact Area	Specific Goal	Method	Timeframe
Education	Fund 3 student scholarships	Set up a donor fund	12 months
Faith/Community	Support a small church in your city	Monthly giving	Ongoing
Family Legacy	Teach financial literacy to children	Host family workshops	Quarterly
Global Missions	Support clean water in Africa	Partner with/ nonprofit	Annually

---

THE BENEFITS OF GIVING

- **Inner fulfillment** – A more profound sense of purpose and peace.
- **Connection** – Real relationships forged through shared values.
- **Eternal reward** – Generosity aligns you with God's heart.
- **Cultural legacy** – Your generosity becomes the new standard for your family.
- **Emotional well-being** – Giving combats isolation and boosts joy.

LEGACY GIVING ACTION STEPS:

1. **Pray and reflect**: Ask God to show you who you're meant to impact.
2. **Create a giving journal**: Record your intentions, gifts, and the testimonies you receive.
3. **Talk with your family**: Include them in the vision.
4. **Set aside a portion**: Establish a "Generosity Fund" in your budget.
5. **Choose one person, one cause, or one mission** to give to this week.

POWERFUL AFFIRMATION:

"I am blessed to be a blessing. My wealth is a tool for impact. I give from a place of abundance, purpose, and joy. My generosity will echo for generations."

SECTION 1: Define Your Target Audience

Answer the following prompts clearly and honestly.

1. Who do you serve best?

→ Describe your ideal customer in detail (age, gender, profession, pain points).

2. What are they struggling with?

→ List their top 3 problems.

3. What do they dream of achieving?

→ List their goals, desires, and outcomes they hope for.

4. What keeps them up at night?

→ Tap into emotional fears and daily frustrations.

5. Where do they spend time (online and offline)?

→ Platforms, communities, podcasts, events, etc.

SECTION 2: Define Your Brand

Clarify the message and identity you're bringing into the world.

1. Brand Mission:

→ What problem do you solve and for whom?

2. Brand Values:

→ What principles guide your message and decisions?

3. Signature Promise:

→ What is the ONE major transformation you offer?

4. Unique Voice/Tone:

→ Are you bold? Warm? Visionary? Direct? Inspiring?

5. Brand Story:

→ Why does this work matter to you? What is your "why"?

SECTION 3: Clarify Your Positioning

Pinpoint what makes your brand valuable and different.

1. Category You Belong To:

→ Example: Mindset Coach, Branding Strategist, Financial Educator

2. Your Differentiator:

→ What makes you *stand out*? Is it your story, method, speed, or transformation?

3. The Payoff:

→ What's the life-changing result your customer will get?

---

25 WAYS TO USE THE BRAND CLARITY MAP

1. Craft your personal elevator pitch
2. Write a compelling "About" page
3. Design brand visuals (logos, colors, fonts)
4. Create targeted Instagram content
5. Build a niche-specific lead magnet
6. Pitch yourself to podcasts
7. Write a confident speaker bio
8. Position yourself as a thought leader in your industry
9. Target the proper Facebook Groups or online communities
10. Develop a transformational coaching program

11. Launch a masterclass for your exact audience
12. Design a homepage that speaks to your people
13. Get clarity before creating a sales funnel
14. Avoid vague messaging in ads and posts
15. Build a loyal email subscriber list
16. Speak directly to your audience in Reels or TikTok
17. Tailor your freebie to your top-performing content
18. Optimize your bio on LinkedIn or IG
19. Align your offers to the most urgent needs
20. Pre-qualify the best clients or customers
21. Create emotional hooks in your messaging
22. Establish a long-term content strategy
23. Develop a brand voice guide for consistency
24. Start building your community with purpose
25. Design high-converting webinars or sales pages

Who Am I Called to Bless?

25 Key Strategies to Create, Build, and Prosper with Purpose

---

1. Define Your "Blessing Zone"

Identify the people whose lives are transformed by your skills, knowledge, or experiences. Define your blessing zone by asking: *Whose life gets better because I show up?*

---

2. Create a Blessing Map

Sketch a visual map of all the groups or individuals you are equipped to serve—family, business clients, local community, global audience.

---

3. Journal Your Blessing Moments

Reflect on the times you've made someone's life easier or better. What were you doing? What came naturally? Use this to discover your gift in motion.

---

4. Interview Your Inner Circle

Ask 3–5 trusted people: *"What do you believe I bring to the world?"* You may be surprised by the patterns they see in how you serve others.

---

5. Solve One Problem for One Person

Blessing begins with one act. Identify one person, one need, and offer one solution. Build from there.

---

6. Design a Solution Around Your Testimony

Use a past struggle or challenge you've overcome as a platform to create a product, service, or message that blesses others in the same situation.

---

7. Create a Signature Message

Develop a one-sentence message that combines your purpose and who you're called to bless. Example: "I help overlooked creators turn their ideas into legacy and income."

---

8. Package Your Blessing

Turn your help into something tangible—a course, book, product, or service that multiplies impact.

9. Teach What You Know

Create workshops, webinars, or small groups around your zone of blessing. Teaching activates confidence and multiplies value.

10. Listen to Pain Points

Talk to people. What are they struggling with? Blessing others begins with solving what hurts them.

11. Build a Blessing-Based Brand

Let your brand messaging reflect who you are called to bless. Speak their language, reflect their struggles, and offer hope.

12. Offer a Free Resource

Create a lead magnet or free mini-course that helps your audience take one small step forward.

13. Develop a Legacy Project

Create something that will outlive you—a foundation, scholarship, mentorship program, or business that continues to bless.

---

14. Serve Consistently in One Area

Commit to one audience, one cause, or one purpose for a defined time—consistency compounds blessing and prosperity.

---

15. Track Impact, Not Just Income

Use testimonials, success stories, and feedback as metrics to track how your blessing is transforming lives.

---

16. Use Your Platform to Uplift Others

Whether social media, a podcast, or a stage—shine a light on the people you serve, not just yourself.

---

17. Create a Giving Goal

Set a financial goal linked to giving (e.g., 10% of profits go to a cause aligned with your calling).

---

18. Mentor Someone

Take someone under your wing. One-on-one impact can ignite confidence and a sense of purpose.

---

19. Launch a Blessing Campaign

Host a 30-day impact challenge. Encourage your community to bless others in return for what they've received from you.

---

20. Document Your Blessing Journey

Blog, vlog, or post your story of service and impact. This builds trust, legacy, and expands reach.

---

21. Ask This Daily Question

Each morning, ask: *"Who am I called to bless today?"* and listen. Keep a running list of people who come to mind.

---

22. Use Feedback to Refine Your Impact

Read every comment, email, and review. Let their language shape your next move.

---

23. Design a Product With Your Audience

Collaborate with those you serve to co-create something they need and want.

---

24. Pray Over Your Business

Align your heart with divine guidance. Blessing multiplies when it flows through a willing and obedient vessel.

---

25. Declare Your Blessing Intention

Write a Blessing Statement:

"I am called to bless [audience] by using my [skill/gift] to help them [solve problem]. I will build, create, and prosper in a way that lifts others while honoring my calling."

Summary:

You prosper by becoming a blessing. These 25 strategies help you take ownership of their purpose, turn their impact into a solution, and build wealth by solving real problems with intention and love.

Bonus Chapter: Creativity Is Currency – The Armor of Riches and Wealth

Welcome to your bonus chapter, where you're not just reminded of your power — you're *armed* with it.

Throughout this book, you've learned to think, create, build, and prosper. Now, it's time to suit up — because *wealth without protection is vulnerable, and creativity without structure drifts.*

The **Armor of Riches and Wealth** is your framework for standing firm, moving smart, and living purposefully. It's both a mindset and a method. It gives you direction *and* defense. It is the set of tools that ensures your ideas don't just inspire — they *multiply.*

The Six Pieces of Armor — A Complete Overview

Each piece represents a vital area of your life and business, working together to help you own your creativity and convert it into lasting impact and wealth.

---

1. Helmet of Identity & Mindset

Purpose: Protects your *thoughts, beliefs, and vision.*
How to Apply:

- Develop a daily habit of affirmations: "I am the creator of value. I own my ideas. I attract opportunity."
- Identify negative thought patterns and replace them with truth-centered beliefs.
- Study examples of creators who overcame adversity — feed your mind daily.

Benchmark Questions:

- Am I thinking like a receiver or a resistor?
- Do I believe wealth is possible for me?

---

2. Breastplate of Skill Set

Purpose: Shields and strengthens your *problem-solving abilities* — the core of your value.
How to Apply:

- List the top three problems you can solve today with your existing skills.
- Take one online course or read a book monthly to sharpen your expertise.
- Package your skill in a way that others can understand and buy.

Benchmark Questions:

- What skill do I possess that people would pay for?

- Am I practicing or perfecting my gift regularly?

---

3. Sword of Branding & Marketing

Purpose: Your *voice in the world.* Branding attracts; marketing persuades.
How to Apply:

- Create your brand identity (name, logo, color theme, and tone).
- Write a clear mission statement: *What do you help people do, and why?*
- Build marketing funnels (including social media, email, and paid advertising) to reach your target audience effectively.

Benchmark Questions:

- Is my brand message consistent and visible?
- Am I speaking directly to a specific problem and person?

---

4. Shoes of Readiness

Purpose: Prepares you to *move quickly and confidently* toward opportunity.
How to Apply:

- Start building your audience TODAY (social media, email list, live sessions).

- Prepare a pitch deck or offer for your product or service.
- Always be ready to present your ideas and value.

Benchmark Questions:

- Do I have something to offer if a client were to show up today?
- Am I consistently sharing my message?

---

5. Belt of Revenue

Purpose: Secures your income with *multiple streams of monetization.*
How to Apply:

- Identify at least three ways to monetize your idea (book sales, courses, coaching, merch).
- Track monthly income and create a budget for reinvestment.
- Develop new offers regularly (every 30–60–90 days).

Benchmark Questions:

- Where is my income currently coming from?
- What new revenue stream can I add this month?

---

6. Shield of Protection

Purpose: Guards your *wealth, reputation, and legacy.*
How to Apply:

- Invest in insurance, asset protection, and legal structures to safeguard your financial interests.
- Begin estate planning — wills, trusts, life insurance.
- Diversify income and investment portfolios for security.

Benchmark Questions:

- Is my wealth protected from risk?
- Have I created a plan for long-term security?

The Diamond at the Center — *YOU, the Creator*

You are the *engine* of this armor. None of it works without your belief, consistency, and commitment. The Armor doesn't just protect your wealth — it *protects your purpose.*

You are called to create.
You are born to build.
You are chosen to lead.

Step-by-Step Action Guide

Day	Task	Purpose
Day 1–2	Write down your vision.	Anchor your identity.
Day 3–4	List three problems you can solve.	Define your skill set.
Day 5–6	Design a simple brand message.	Clarify your sword.
Day 7–8	Build one platform to connect (social/email).	Prepare your shoes.
Day 9–10	Create one offer and pricing.	Buckle your belt.
Day 11–12	Research asset protection basics.	Raise your shield.
Day 13+	Begin combining and applying these daily.	Walk fully armored.

ARMOR OF RICHES AND WEALTH

Practical Strategies to Prosper With Your Ideas

---

1. Sword of Branding & Marketing

Purpose: Position your idea powerfully in the marketplace.

1. **Define Your Brand Identity** – Write your brand story and what makes you different.

2. **Create a Strong Visual Identity** – Design a logo, choose your brand colors, and maintain consistent design across all platforms.
3. **Build a Signature Message** – Develop a powerful tagline and pitch that reflects your values and the unique offer you provide.
4. **Create Targeted Content** – Make content that speaks directly to your ideal audience's needs and desires.
5. **Develop a Content Marketing Plan – Utilize blogs, videos, and social media posts to demonstrate** thought leadership and establish your brand as a thought leader.

---

2. Shoes of Readiness

Purpose: Prepare to walk confidently in your mission.

1. **Identify Your Ideal Audience** – Build a customer avatar with detailed pain points and desires.
2. **Create a Problem-Solving Product or Service** – Ensure your offer addresses a deep emotional or practical need.
3. **Prepare Your Product for Sale** – Get feedback, revise, and make it user-friendly.
4. **Build an Email List Early** – Capture leads with a free resource or workbook.
5. **Practice Your Sales Pitch** – Get comfortable explaining what you do and why it matters.

---

3. Belt of Revenue

Purpose: Secure income streams and deliver real value.

1. **Design Multiple Income Streams** – Courses, coaching, digital products, physical goods, licensing, etc.
2. **Create a Pricing Strategy** – Tier your offerings for accessibility and value.
3. **Launch a Pre-Sale or Waiting List** – Build anticipation and get early buyers.
4. **Track Financial Performance** – Use simple tools like Excel, QuickBooks, or Notion templates.
5. **Develop Repeat Offers** – Subscription, membership, or recurring billing models.

---

4. Shield of Protection

Purpose: Preserve your wealth, assets, and peace of mind.

1. **Get Legal Protection** – File an LLC and trademark your name, logo, or slogan.
2. **Open Separate Business and Personal Accounts – Keep business and personal finances distinct**.
3. **Set Up Insurance** – Liability, Health, and Property Coverage.
4. **Build a Financial Emergency Plan** – Reserve fund for downturns or slow seasons.
5. **Diversify Revenue** – So you're not dependent on one stream.

5. Sword of Skill Set

Purpose: Refine your abilities to deliver value and solve problems.

1. **Learn One High-Income Skill** – Copywriting, public speaking, marketing, branding, etc.
2. **Create a Signature Framework** – Teach what you know using your unique process.
3. **Host Free Workshops** – Get practice and showcase your knowledge.
4. **Join a Mastermind or Coaching Group** – Surround yourself with people who challenge you.
5. **Continuously Learn & Improve** – Stay at the forefront of industry trends.

THE OUTCOME:

When applied consistently:

- Activate the creator within you.
- Establish a visible and credible presence.
- Attract the right audience.
- Generate multiple streams of revenue.
- Protect what you've built.
- Create long-term wealth from your creativity.

The Wealth Warrior's Commitment

"I commit to wearing the Armor of Riches and Wealth daily.
I commit to protecting my mind, cultivating my value, and sharing my gifts with bold confidence.
I choose creativity. I choose discipline. I choose wealth.
I will build. I will rise. I will leave a legacy."

Closing Remarks: The Power is Already in You

Dear Reader,

As you close this book, know this: you are no longer the same person who opened these pages.

You have traveled through a journey of insight, inspiration, and transformation. You've uncovered the truth that your ideas are not small; they are seeds of greatness. You've realized that your creativity is not random—it is powerfully placed within you for a purpose.

The time is now. The world isn't waiting for you to get it perfect—it's waiting for you to get started.

Your hands hold the power to build a legacy.
Your mind holds the blueprint.
And your heart holds the reason why.

The tools, the strategies, and the mindset have been placed before you. What happens next is your move. **You were born to create. You were born to contribute. You were born to own your creativity.**

You have walked through fire to build what you now hold. Don't let your legacy end with accumulation. Let it begin with multiplication, through giving.

Your wealth is more than what you keep. It's also what you give.

"Legacy is not what you leave ***for*** *people. It's what you leave* **in** *them."*

— David Toliver

Chapter One: Creativity Activation

Creativity Is Currency: Activation

Guided by Chapter One: "What's in Your Hands Today?"

Purpose:
This helps you identify your current reality, shift from limited beliefs to empowered beliefs, adopt a creator mindset, and begin putting on the Armor of Riches and Wealth. It's a personal roadmap to *activate your creativity, claim ownership of your ideas,* and *take your first step toward wealth and purpose.*

Section 1: Limited Beliefs → Empowered Beliefs

Instructions: Write down your current limiting belief in the left column. In the right column, write an empowered belief to replace it.

Limited Belief I Hold	Empowered Belief I Choose to Embrace
I'm not creative enough.	My creativity is a unique and valuable gift.
I don't have enough resources.	I can create with what I already have.
I'm afraid to fail	Every step forward builds my future.

➡ Reflection Prompt:
Which belief has held you back the most, and how will you begin challenging it this week?

Section 2: Riches vs. Wealth

Definitions Recap:

- *Riches* = Money, material possessions, temporary gain
- *Wealth* = Purpose, legacy, creativity, long-term impact

Prompt:
What have you been chasing—riches or wealth? What shift do you feel called to make?

Write Your Wealth Commitment Statement:
"I will build wealth by..." (Finish this sentence)

Section 3: Embracing the Creator Mindset

The Creator Mindset means you believe:

- You are the source, not just a consumer.
- You take responsibility for your life.
- You can turn ideas into value.

Answer the following:

1. What's one idea or skill you already have that could solve a problem for others?
2. Who would benefit from this idea, and how?
3. What small step can you take this week to *create* something from this idea?

Section 4: The Armor of Riches and Wealth

Put on the Armor!

Match each piece of armor with one action you'll take this month:

Armor Piece	Action You Will Take This Month
Helmet of Belief (Mindset)	
Sword of Skill Set	
Breastplate of Branding	
Shoes of Readiness (Offer Creation)	
Belt of Revenue	
Shield of Protection	

➡ Reflection Prompt:

Which piece of armor do you feel least equipped with right now? What's one thing you can do to strengthen it?

Progress & Activation Tracker

Track Your Weekly Progress:

Week	Goal/Action	Progress	Notes
1	____________________	☐ Not Started ☐ In Progress ☐ Done	____________________
2	____________________	☐ Not Started ☐ In Progress ☐ Done	____________________
3	____________________	☐ Not Started ☐ In Progress ☐ Done	____________________
4	____________________	☐ Not Started ☐ In Progress ☐ Done	____________________

Final Reflection:

"What's in your hands today?"

Make a list of resources, skills, relationships, or passions you already have:

- ____
- ____
- ____

Now answer:
How will you use what you already have to create something valuable in the next 30 days?

Ready for Activation?

Please take a photo or screenshot of your completed and post it to your journal, group, or personal space. Declare:
"I am activated. I am a creator. I own my creativity."

Chapter Two: Wisdom Tracker

Creativity Is Currency: Wisdom Tracker

Chapter Focus: The Power of Wisdom in Wealth

"Wealth does not create wisdom—but wisdom can create wealth."

SECTION 1: Personal Wisdom Inventory

Rate yourself from 1–5 on the following areas of personal wisdom:
(1 = Needs Growth, 5 = Strong)

Wisdom Area	Score (1–5)	Notes/Reflection
Long-Term Thinking		
Financial Discernment		
Emotional Control in Decision-Making		
Ability to Learn from Past Mistakes		
Willingness to Seek Counsel		
Making Value-Aligned Decisions		

Journal Prompt:

Where do you notice patterns in your decision-making that don't align with wisdom?

SECTION 2: Weekly Wisdom Activation Plan

Use this section to create weekly actions that help you **apply wisdom** in your finances, business, and life.

Week	Focus Area	Action Step	Why It Matters to Me	Result
1	Financial Decisions	Delay a significant purchase for 72 hours	Avoid impulse decisions	

Week	Focus Area	Action Step	Why It Matters to Me	Result
2	Time Management	Review your calendar and remove one time-waster	Increase productivity for clarity	
3	Relationships	Ask a mentor or coach for advice	Gain insight from trusted voices	
4	Business Decisions	Compare the short vs. long-term impact of the choice	Build sustainable wealth	

Customize the action steps to fit your journey.

SECTION 3: Reflection & Realignment

Reflection Questions:

1. What was one moment this week when I used wisdom instead of emotion?
2. How has practicing wisdom impacted my clarity and confidence?
3. In what area of life am I tempted to act impulsively or without reflection?
4. What are three wisdom habits I want to build?

SECTION 4: Wisdom + Wealth Benchmark Chart

Track the visible results of wisdom applied to your life and business:

Area of Growth	Before Applying Wisdom	After 30 Days of Wisdom Practice	Notes on Progress
Finances			
Time Use			
Decision-Making			
Emotional Clarity			

SECTION 5: Wisdom Creed (Affirmation)

"I choose wisdom over impulse. I choose vision over noise. My decisions today shape my legacy tomorrow. I am a steward of insight, and wisdom is the foundation of my wealth."

Sign Here to Commit to the Journey: ___________________________

Date: ____________________

Chapter Four: Build Your Financial Wisdom Circle

Build Your Financial Wisdom Circle

"Your ideas are the source of your wealth, but wisdom is what makes that wealth sustainable." — David Toliver.

SECTION ONE: DISCOVER YOURSELF

Chapter Focus: Self-Awareness is the Foundation

1. What Do You Believe About Wealth?

- What did you grow up believing about money?
- What limiting beliefs do you hold about wealth today?
- How do your beliefs affect your current financial behaviors?

Reflection Box:
I used to believe... Now I believe...

SECTION TWO: DEFINE YOUR VALUES

Chapter Focus: Clarity Before Prosperity

List your top five core life values. Now, compare them to how you spend money and time.

- Are your values aligned with your financial behavior?
- What needs to change?

Core Value Tracker:

Core Value	Does your spending reflect this?	How will you adjust?

SECTION THREE: WISDOM IN ACTION

"Wealth doesn't create wisdom. Wisdom creates wealth."

Define your Financial Wisdom Circle (Who/What Influences You?)

1. **Who do you go to for wise financial advice?**
2. **What books or tools have transformed your mindset?**
3. **What lessons has life taught you about money?**
4. **What mistakes have made you wiser?**

Build Your Circle (Add names/tools/experiences):

People	Books/Resources	Lessons Learned	Actions Moving Forward

SECTION FOUR: CREATE YOUR INNER BOARDROOM

Become the person who can receive, manage, and multiply wealth.

You are the CEO of your financial future.

Select your **Inner Advisors**:

- **The Visionary**: Your future self
- **The Analyst**: Tracks numbers/data
- **The Counselor**: Focuses on values/morals
- **The Creator**: Thinks in opportunities

Create a scenario:

A significant financial decision lies in front of you. How would each Inner Advisor respond?

SECTION FIVE: BENCHMARKING YOUR WISDOM

Use this benchmark chart to assess your current level of financial wisdom:

Benchmark Area	Low	Medium	High	Notes for Growth
Self-Awareness				
Strategic Thinking				
Emotional Discipline				
Long-Term Planning				
Value-Based Spending				

SECTION SIX: WISDOM-DRIVEN DECISION MAKING

"Wisdom leads you to make decisions that protect your future, not just satisfy the present."

Scenario:

You receive a surprise $10,000.
What would **wisdom tell you to do**?

- What's your first reaction?
- What's your most responsible response?
- How can this align with your values and wealth goals?

Write Your Wise Response:

SECTION SEVEN: BUILD YOUR DAILY PRACTICE

Wealth is built daily. Wisdom is applied in every decision.

Create a 7-Day Wisdom Practice Challenge

Day	Action	Reflection
1	Listen to a financial podcast.	
2	Read a chapter of a wealth-building book.	
3	Track every dollar you spend	

Day	Action	Reflection
4	Ask someone wise a financial question.	
5	Journal your money story.	
6	Share a money tip with someone younger.	
7	Meditate on your financial goals.	

A COMPELLING THOUGHT:

"When wisdom becomes your financial compass, your creativity becomes unstoppable." — David Toliver

Use this monthly. Update your wisdom circle, revisit your benchmarks, and grow from your experiences. Your ideas are powerful—but paired with wisdom, they become unstoppable engines of wealth.

Chapter Six: The Legacy Builder Blueprint

Legacy Builder Blueprint

Based on Chapter Five: Riches Are Not Forever

INTRODUCTION

You are building something that will outlast you.
This helps you activate the **legacy mindset**. Use it to identify your values, build a long-term plan, and transfer wisdom and wealth to the next generation.

STEP 1: CLARIFY YOUR LEGACY VISION

Reflect: What does legacy mean to you?
Write 2-3 sentences describing the legacy you want to leave behind.

Legacy Vision Statement:

Write Down

STEP 2: EDUCATE YOUR FAMILY ABOUT MONEY

✓ *Checklist for Financial Family Education:*

Action	Completed (✓)
Have you taught your family the basics of budgeting?	
Have you had open conversations about debt/saving?	
Do you involve your children or spouse in financial	

Action	Completed (✓)
decisions?	
Have you created financial roles or responsibilities?	
Have you discussed the concept of **earned** vs **inherited** wealth?	

Benchmark: *Family members should be able to articulate their core values around money.*

STEP 3: DIVERSIFY & INVEST WISELY

Diversification Matrix

Income Source	Is it Active or Passive?	Diversified? (Y/N)	Priority to Improve
Your Business			
Real Estate			
Stock Portfolio			
Life Insurance/770 Plan			
Royalties (Book, IP)			

Goal: Create **at least three income streams** that grow with or without your effort.

STEP 4: PLAN FOR GENERATIONAL TRANSFER

Checklist: Estate & Legacy Planning

Action	Completed (✓)
Will or Trust Created	
Power of Attorney Established	
Life Insurance in Place	
Beneficiaries Updated	
770 Account or Legacy Account in Place	
Estate Attorney or Financial Planner Consulted	
Family Meeting Scheduled to Discuss Plans	

Notes:

____

____

STEP 5: SURROUND YOURSELF WITH WISE COUNSEL

Who are your trusted advisors?

Name	Role (Financial, Legal, Mentor, etc.)	Trusted? (Y/N)

If you don't have a team, start building one.

MILESTONE TRACKER

30-Day Goal

Write one milestone you want to achieve in 30 days.

___

60-Day Goal

___

90-Day Goal

DIAMOND OF LEGACY FRAMEWORK

In the center is **YOU** (The Creator). Around you are your 4 Legacy Pillars:

[Wise Counsel]

▲

|

[Invest Wisely] ◄— YOU —► [Educate Family]

|

▼

[Generational Transfer]

Purpose: You're not building income. You're building **impact**.
Every action you take today writes the story of your family's future.

Reflection

What's one habit you must start TODAY to protect your legacy?

What must you stop doing that puts your legacy at risk?

Chapter Do It With All Your Might Action Map

Creativity Is Currency: Do It With All Your Might Activation

PURPOSE:

To help you take decisive, bold action toward their purpose, wealth, and creative potential by doing it all with your MIGHT. This is structured to ignite personal transformation and measurable progress.

CENTRAL THEME:

Do It With All Your Might = Wholehearted Action + Creative Confidence + Strategic Generosity

---

Section 1: "Where Are You Right Now?"

Reflection Prompt	Your Response
What dream or idea have you been putting off?	
What resources (skills, knowledge, network) do you already have?	
What is your biggest excuse?	
How will your life change if you act today?	

Section 2: The MIGHT Framework

MIGHT Component	What It Means	Personal Action
M – Maximize your mindset	Challenge all limiting beliefs.	
I – Invest your time & effort.	Focus daily on your top 3 priorities.	
G – Give with purpose	Identify where your gift can meet a need.	
H – Hold yourself accountable	Share your plan with a mentor or coach.	
T – Take massive action	What will you execute in the next 72 hours?	

Progress Tracker (Benchmark Your Momentum)

Week	Goal	Completed?	Notes
Week 1	Write your product or service idea.	✓ / X	
Week 2	Create your first offer.	✓ / X	
Week 3	Share your story or post online.	✓ / X	
Week 4	Serve or sell with confidence.	✓ / X	

Diamond of Action: Personal Activation Map

Draw or visualize yourself at the center of the square.

Quadrant	Focus	Action
Top Left	**Creativity**	What will you create this month?
Top Right	**Generosity**	Who will benefit from your gift?
Bottom Left	**Discipline**	What new daily habit will you start?
Bottom Right	**Execution**	What deadline will you hit this week?

Urgency Activation:

Answer these:

1. What will it cost you to keep waiting?
2. Who suffers when you delay your purpose?
3. What are you willing to give up to go all in?

Pledge:

"I will no longer wait for perfect conditions. I am ready. I am equipped. I will do it with all my might — starting NOW."

Call to Action:

Write a bold action plan for the next 24 hours:

I will...

BONUS: Empowerment Checklist

I have identified my current reality

I have broken my goal into actions

I have committed to daily execution

I've shared my commitment with someone

I am acting with all my MIGHT

"Don't wait. What you own today can fund your tomorrow." – David Toliver.

Purpose of the Toolkit

To turn inspiration into tangible success by giving you the benchmarks, tools, and charts they need to act on the wisdom from your book — chapter by chapter — and **build their creative wealth strategy.**

TOOLKIT OVERVIEW

Chapter	Core Action	Activity	Benchmark/Chart
1. What's in Your Hands Today	Identify your current skills and assets	Inventory: "Skill Set & Creativity Audit"	Pie Chart: How you use your time vs. where your skills lie
2. Wisdom for the Journey	Make wise, informed decisions	"Wisdom vs. Impulse" Decision Tree	Compass Chart: Short-term vs. Long-term Thinking
3. Becoming the Receiver	Shift identity to one who receives	"Identity Alignment Reflection"	Timeline of Mindset Shift
4. Creative Power & The Wealth Plan	Build a system from your ideas	"Wealth Blueprint Sketch"	S.T.A.R.T. Framework (See below)
5. Branding and Identity	Clarify brand and voice	"Your Brand Voice & Logo Map"	Visual Brand Pyramid
6. Income & Impact	Generate and track revenue	"Revenue Stream Brainstorm"	Revenue Streams Tracker
7. Legacy & Generosity	Commit to a purpose beyond profit	"Legacy Letter to Self"	Giving & Growth Timeline

THE "S.T.A.R.T." FRAMEWORK

Every idea must S.T.A.R.T. to become profitable:

- **S** – Sketch it out
- **T** – Test it quickly
- **A** – Align it with a real need
- **R** – Refine the value
- **T** – Take it to market

Call to Action:

- "What are three things in your hands today that could become products?"
- "Write the name of someone you could help right now with your creativity."
- "Sketch your wealth system. What does it look like in motion?"
- "Write your future legacy in one paragraph."

TARGET AUDIENCE & BRAND CLARITY MAP

- **Purpose:** Helps you align your unique creativity with the right audience and present their brand with confidence, clarity, and value.

Appendix: Tools, Resources & Study Aids

You now have the blueprint to build wealth. Now build worth. You've gained power. Now give a purpose. You've walked your journey. Now light the way for someone else.

The world is waiting for your generosity. Don't delay. You are the answer to someone's prayer. Let your legacy begin today.

Now go—be the light. Be the answer. Be the blessing.

Your Guide to Deepen the Journey, Multiply Your Impact, and Leave a Legacy

A. Recommended Reading & Resources

Books That Expand Your Wealth, Wisdom, and Leadership Mindset

The book: **www.theempoweredcreators.com.com/book**

2. Free Introduction Class: **www.theempoweredcreators.com/starter**

3. $99 Signature Class **www.theempoweredcreators.com/blueprint**

4. $5,000 Premium Progress **www.theempoweredcreators.com/legacy**

5. $10,000 Elite Offer **www.theempoweredcreators.com/accelerator**

https://www.theempoweredcreators.com/creative-ideas-into-cash
https://www.theempoweredcreators.com/workbook

Scan the QR Code Below to Get *Creativity Is Currency: How To Turn Your Ideas Into Wealth*

www.ingramcontent.com/pod-product-compliance
Lightning Source LLC
LaVergne TN
LVHW082334200926
848481LV00012B/3348

* 9 7 9 8 3 4 9 5 8 7 6 7 2 *